PENGUIN BOOKS

THE PENGUIN BOOK OF GAMES

Sarah Toynbee, one of six sisters, was born in Oxford and brought up there and in North Yorkshire.

She has worked in publishing, television, radio and newspapers. She now lives in West London with her husband and two small children.

THE PENGUIN BOOK OF GAMES

SARAH TOYNBEE

PENGUIN BOOKS

PENGUIN BOOKS

Published by the Penguin Group
Penguin Books Ltd, 27 Wrights Lane, London w8 5tz, England
Penguin Books USA Inc., 375 Hudson Street, New York, New York 10014, USA
Penguin Books Australia Ltd, Ringwood, Victoria, Australia
Penguin Books Canada Ltd, 10 Alcorn Avenue, Toronto, Ontario, Canada m4v 3b2
Penguin Books (NZ) Ltd, 182–190 Wairau Road, Auckland 10, New Zealand

Penguin Books Ltd, Registered Offices: Harmondsworth, Middlesex, England

First published 1993
10 9 8 7 6 5 4 3 2 1

Typeset by Datix International Limited, Bungay, Suffolk
Filmset in 10/12 pt Monophoto Bembo
Printed in England by Clays Ltd, St Ives plc

To RCT

CONTENTS

CHAPTER 3
QUICK THINKING

CHAPTER 4
PENCIL AND PAPER

CHAPTER 5
LATE NIGHT AND BOISTEROUS

ACKNOWLEDGEMENTS

Games are sociable, and people not only play them together but share variations and new games with one another. Finding out whether a newly discovered game is all it has been cracked up to be is as much fun as playing one which is tried and tested. And so this compilation, in common with every other, contains games from a multitude of people and places. To attempt a full list of sources and a complete account of debts would be foolish since some contributions would go unacknowledged and some would be misleadingly attributed. A couple of examples must suffice. Who? Who? came from John Slater, who, like me, got it from Anthony Blond, who I believe invented it. Pub Cricket was contributed by Tom Hibbert, who says that he and his father Christopher made it up on long car journeys when Tom was a boy.

All I can do, in fairness, is say how very grateful I am to my friends for the many conversations we have had about this book while it was in the making, and for their generosity in letting me use their ideas so freely. Thank you.

The one exception must be Jane Charteris. She and I have played games together since we were children and it was her help and encouragement which got the book completed. To her therefore I owe a special debt of thanks.

The publishers would like to thank Maureen Lipman for permission to quote from her book *When's It Coming Out?* (London: Robson Books, 1992).

INTRODUCTION

Usually, games are equated with children, but this is a book of games for everyone *except* children (although, of course, there are many they will enjoy). In fact, we all play games, and we play them at all ages. We play them as babies; we play them with our families and our friends; we play them as grown-ups – often more seriously than we intend to – and we play them by ourselves, from the cradle to the grave and at every stage between. A clever Dutchman even wrote a book called *Homo Ludens* which said that playing games was the very essence of being human.

This is a practical book of games, in which I describe some of the games I have enjoyed playing with my friends and other people. The important word is *enjoy*, for that is the point of games. If you try one of these games and do not have fun then try another at once, for the only point of playing a game is that everyone involved should enjoy themselves.

I have grouped this hundred or so games under chapter headings but perhaps I should give you a more general guide to the kind of games I have included.

First, there are the games which involve thinking and puzzling. We all have reflective moments when these are the games to enjoy, but sometimes they are perfect for playing with one or two friends when the crowds are screaming around on something more boisterous.

Then there are the games of pure innocence, suitable for children of all ages. These involve neither thinking nor cleverness nor deviousness. Very few grown-ups are capable of enjoying them without the presence of children, but perhaps they are the best of all – look up Good Morning, Madam.

At the opposite extreme are the games of experience, some of which will tax the ingenuity of the most sophisticated player. Games such as In the Manner of the Word are suited equally to market makers and street traders, and even truly resourceful people will find them challenging.

And then there are the games which are just plain silly – and delightful. These demand a crowd of players, of whom at least some should be friends, and of whom almost all should be unfit to drive a motor car.

Finally, there are games for only really grown-up players – those in which people make fools of themselves and of each other.

Some people play games as though by second nature, and some need to be encouraged gently into the fun. I have played all of these games, and though I am hardly an extrovert (though certainly an expert) I have enjoyed each one of them. So can you.

CHAPTER 1

CAR GAMES

It's Friday evening, spirits are high, four of you are off on a long car journey. Within about forty minutes and with still hundreds of miles to go, you've exhausted conversation, gossip has become repetitive, Radio 4 is an irritating crackle, Radio 1 is simply irritating, you don't want to listen to Dire Straits or sing along any more to Dusty or Tammy – *anything* but that . . . Let's face it, you are bored. What do you do?

You play one of the many hugely entertaining games designed for just such circumstances. Some are noisy, some less so; some require a degree of thought, others none whatsoever; some will be familiar as adaptations of parlour games, others rely on the invention of the motor car; some are perfect for the motorways, some for B roads, yet others for traffic jams.

A selection of any six will afford a car-load of teenagers to ninetysomethings miles and miles' worth of amusement.

Botticelli

A game that appeals to know-it-alls of all ages, Botticelli can inspire passionate arguments among participants, starting with its name: those who played it before 'the war' call it The Box, presumably because one player is interrogated by the others.

Any number of people can play. One person announces the surname initial of a famous character, real or fictional, whom he has thought of, such as M (for Mozart). The other players then think of other famous people whose names begin with M and, taking it in turns, ask *indirect* questions about these characters, in an attempt to catch out the person in 'the box'.

Example

Player One: I begin with M.

Player Two: Are you an actress reputed to have had an affair with John F. Kennedy?

Player One: I am not Marilyn Monroe.

Player Three: Are you a character in *The Naked Lunch*?

Player One: I am not . . . I am not . . . oh God, it's so long since I read any Norman Mailer . . .

Player Three: Norman Mailer didn't write *The Naked Lunch*. You obviously don't know that you are not a Mugwump. I'll have a direct question, thank you.

Direct questions are the way into Player One's character. They must be phrased in such a way as only to be answered by 'Yes' or 'No'. For example, 'Are you alive?' (People, even of quite advanced years, often ask, 'Are you alive or dead?', 'Are you male or female?', although these are not answerable by yes or no, and it should be quite obvious the alternative is implicit.) 'Are/were you in the arts/politics/crime/etc.?' 'Are you Mozart?' (It is usually advisable to wait until you have some information before asking this most direct of questions.)

Direct questions must be answered truthfully. However, if Player One is asked indirectly, 'Did you write *The Magic Flute*?', he can say, 'I am not Mozart', even if he is. Younger players often get very worked up over this rule, so it is important to explain as clearly as possible the difference between direct and indirect questions. Player One cannot change his mind half-way through about who he is.

The art of indirect questioning lies in being specific or oblique. Do not ask blanket questions, such as 'Are you a composer?' Although as questioner you are allowed to repeat it three times, it gives Player One such scope, you are unlikely to win a direct question. Therefore, attach a century, a nationality or anything else that narrows the field. Even better, make the question oblique, i.e. not 'Are you an actor who became a US President?', but 'Are you the star of *Bedtime for Bonzo*?' This way you win more direct questions with which to catch your man, and a broad general knowledge comes in very useful here. Unfortunately it is also where the arguments start. 'That's unfair/ too difficult . . .', and so on. Be tough.

If you are in 'the box', do try to choose a character you know something about. It can cause extreme bad temper among the others if you don't know the answer to simple direct questions, such as 'Are you nineteenth century?'

Disagreements also arise when the age of the group of players varies too greatly. A twelve-year-old who chooses to be Raphael will probably be thinking of a cartoon turtle, of whom his grandmother of The Box generation will never have heard. He, on the other hand, will probably not know a whole heap about Italian painters.

Botticelli is endlessly adaptable. To speed it along you can impose conditions, such as so many questions have to be asked in the next ten miles. It can be played in swimming pools, while out for a walk, in the small hours after a good dinner (though the standard of questioning has been known to deteriorate under these conditions: I was once asked if I was a Scandinavian vegetable, to which I was truthfully able to reply, 'I am not a Swede').

But a long car journey concentrates the mind wonderfully.

Scissors, Paper, Stone

'Everybody knows how to play this!' I hear you cry.

True, but have you thought to play it when trapped in a ten-mile tailback? It quickly succeeds in distracting passengers from their helpless predicament and redirects the frustration that was previously and loudly vented by shouting obscenities at smug radio announcers who delight in telling you that you're stuck in a ten-mile tailback.

In hot traffic jams, car windows rolled down to prevent internal combustion, it can even be played inter-vehicle. I once staggered a game over at least six miles, playing with the occupants of the adjacent car whenever we drew alongside each other. God alone knows what other drivers thought as they saw fists, fingers and hands erupting from car windows over and over again, without a blow ever being exchanged.

Just in case there remains someone who doesn't know the rules (which, I agree, is as unlikely as there being someone who doesn't know who Madonna is), here they are.

Each player puts one hand behind his back and at the count of three brings it out as scissors (two fingers extended); paper (flat hand); or stone (hand in a fist). Scissors score over paper because they can cut it, paper scores over stone because it can wrap it and stone scores over scissors because it can blunt them. When traffic rolls again, drivers should be discouraged from joining in.

The Bum Game or *My Granny's Knickers*

This was taught to me by a television producer on the way up to Yorkshire – four of us played it all the way up the A1 and then for the whole weekend. It is very simple. All you have to do is to think up book titles, film titles, quotations, proverbs or anything like that and replace one word with the word 'bum': for example, 'Bum With the Wind', 'To Kill a Mocking Bum', 'A bum in the hand is worth two in the bush', 'A bum, a bum, my kingdom for a bum' (or 'A horse, a horse, my bum for a horse'), 'Anne of Green Bums', and so on. Try it – it can get obsessive.

I have been told of another version played by my parents' generation when they were young which is to

4

The Bum Game or *My Granny's Knickers*

substitute 'My Granny's Knickers' for a phrase rather than a word (for example, 'To Kill My Granny's Knickers'). Somehow, this is nowhere near as satisfying.

Number-plates

There is one thing you will see a lot of while driving – number-plates, and there are various ways you can use them in games. (This does not take into account I-Spy, the tedium of which can only be alleviated by spying phrases instead of words, such as, Ugly New Town, Redheads In A Fiesta.)

One way is to take the letters from number-plates around you and try to make words out of them: for example, H(855) XGO = HeXaGOn. Opinions vary about how many extra letters you're allowed, but a good rule of thumb is not more than the number-plate contains.

You can also create witty headlines from the letters in

the number-plates: for example, H(855) MCO becomes Hideous Major in College Orgy (little connecting words, like 'in', 'of', 'and', do not have to be represented by a letter in the number-plate). For maximum entertainment use names of fellow passengers or mutual friends.

Obviously, both these games are most fun in fast-moving traffic. They can get a little dull in jams. Some people are mad enough to play these games by themselves.

Number-plate Cricket

A more sophisticated way of using number-plates is this scoring game, which requires some concentration. In-depth knowledge of cricket is not essential, but those who can get to grips with the rudiments of that oh-so-English game might appreciate it more.

This is best played while travelling along a motorway with at least four people in a car. Each player has a full cricket team, i.e. eleven wickets. The first 'batsman' scores by looking out for the numbers 1, 2, 3, 4 or 6 as registered on *one* number-plate around you. So, if he sees RLK 243W, he scores 9 runs, and play moves on to the next person.

However, if the car's number-plate shows a 5, the other players can appeal for 'out': if the next number-plate shows a 7, 8 or 9, a wicket falls. If it shows no 7, 8 or 9, the player is *not* out, and can use the next number-plate to score.

Two adjacent 5s means automatic dismissal – you must *walk*.

Three adjacent 5s loses a player three wickets – a very rare occurrence.

London to Oxford would be good for a one-day inter-national, London to Birmingham should be good for a full test, and London to Tobermory for a full Ashes series.

I Love My Love

This game is far more fun if you spice it up by loving your love because of his or her ghastly attributes, rather than for the conventional syrupy ones, such as, adorable, beautiful, cuddly.

One by one, players complete the sentence 'I love my love because he/she is . . .' following the alphabet from A to Z. So:

'I love my love because she is aggressive.'
'I love my love because he is bossy.'
'I love my love because she is cruel.'
'I love my love because he is doltish.'

And so on, until you love your love because he has zits . . .

If the miles are slipping by almost unnoticed, and you haven't all gone to sleep, you might try another round, this time supplying an adverb and an adjective, such as 'awfully adulterous', 'brassily British', 'coldly candid' . . . Failure to come up with an acceptable description of the by now unspeakable object of your affections dispatches you from the game.

Ghosts

Although often played in the past as a parlour game, with dictionary to hand, this is perfectly suited to our car-bound modern world.

As many people as you can fit in the car may play. One player says a letter, the next in turn, thinking of a word, adds another, and so on in strict left-to-right order around the car. The object is to avoid being the player to complete an English word of more than three letters. Players have three lives, on the loss of the first becoming a third of a ghost, then two-thirds, and finally a full ghost.

A player whose turn it is to call may instead challenge the previous player to supply the word he was thinking of. If the challenged player fails to comply, he loses a life; if the challenge is unsuccessful, the challenger loses. Lives are also lost when a player completes a word. At the end of any round the next player starts anew.

Once you have become a full ghost you may not join fully in the game by calling letters. However, you may noisily haunt the living in an attempt to get one of them to speak to you. If you succeed, the tricked player joins you in the Other World immediately. Full ghosts may talk to each other as much as they like. The lone survivor, when all others have 'moved over', is the winner.

Bluffing is an important element of the game: a player may have no idea of the word the called letters are building up to, but he can still confidently call a letter. It is important to establish that *only* the player whose turn it is next may issue a challenge. Similarly, players must not give their words away by muttering or mouthing them – it is of needless assistance to your opponents.

It may be necessary, even in a car, to establish some 'house' rules, particularly as regards the degree of spooking ghosts may indulge in. While a poltergeist may be acceptable in a house, pinching and throwing things is definitely out of place in a car.

FORE AND AFT

A variation which allows letters to be added at the beginning or end of a group of letters. For example, if the letters called so far spelt AGREEABL, in the normal game the next player would be forced to add the E. In Fore and Aft, he may add an S at the beginning, aiming for DISAGREE-ABLE (but watch out that you don't self-vaporize).

First and Last or Grab on Behind

This is simple but it has to be played fast. Five seconds should be the maximum for thinking. Players decide on categories such as countries, birds, flowers, etc. The first player shouts out a word in the chosen category (for example, birds) and chooses the first word. The next player follows on with a word beginning with the last letter of the previous word . . . and so it goes on. Sparrow becomes Wren becomes Nightingale becomes Egret becomes Turkey becomes . . .

Of course, if all passengers are literary they might choose characters from fiction as a category, although I wouldn't advise it. It can lead to *serious* cheating: 'Oh, she was the maid in Richardson's *Clarissa*. Surely you knew that?' Soap operas are equally dangerous. Drinks are even more notorious for bringing the game into disrepute, since names of cocktails are largely unverifiable.

Initial Letters

One player puts a question, the sillier the better, to any other person in the car, such as 'What do you find sexy?' The responder has to answer with words beginning with his initials. S.A. Turner might answer, 'Slippery Alcoholic Tongues', P.J. Muir might say, 'Puerile Juvenile Maidens' and R. Barrowclough, 'Rounded Buttocks'. Suit your questions to your passengers. It passes the time wonderfully while still allowing for normal conversation.

Initial Answers

The first player thinks of any letter in the alphabet, say B. He then thinks of a three-letter word beginning with B and gives a definition, as in 'B plus two letters is what you can put on a horse.' Any other player can guess the word (bet) and then try to make a four-letter word beginning with B, defining it as, say, 'B plus three letters is what you're supposed to get on when you're looking for work' (bike), and so on. As players fail either to guess the word or to think of another, they drop out until only one person is left.

This game can be played with three lives apiece.

Call of the Wild

This is very silly, noisy game, and it's very funny too. It's really an in-car version of Animal Snap (see p. 61), but the driver should not participate *under any circumstances*.

Call of the Wild

Each player chooses an animal call to imitate, then on 'Go' everyone taps their knees with their hands three times. On the fourth go they show one, two or three fingers. If two players are showing the same number of fingers, they try to be the first to make the *other's* animal noise.

Drivers often call a halt to this game just as the players are really getting into full cry: a carful of farmyard noises can be very distracting. Don't be surprised if you get some odd looks from passing vehicles.

Taboo

There are two versions to this game, one slightly harder than the other. The easier way is to choose a word which comes up often in conversation and once agreed upon by all players this word then becomes 'Taboo'. The word could be 'and', 'the' or 'I'. One player then questions the others and tries to make them say the taboo word. The more difficult version makes a letter taboo and every word which contains it has to be avoided. When a player fails or hesitates too long, he is out and becomes the question master.

This is good for jams and night driving when you can't see Number-plates (see p. 5).

Limericks

Some people are brilliant at composing rhymes off the top of their bonces, others are not. If you fall into the latter category – drive, shut up and appreciate.

It can be either a solo effort, in that one person comes up with the entire limerick, or a team game, with players taking a line each. Either way it is very simple. As you see signposts to towns and villages, make up limericks for them. For example:

> There was a young priest from Lynn
> Who used to be thin as a pin.
> On discovering sweets
> And fine roasted meats
> He took to a life of sin.

> There was a large family from York
> Of whom there was very much talk.
> They didn't have cash
> Or even much dash
> But boy! did they wiggle and walk!

> A family who lived in Clovelly
> Lamented the lack of a telly.
> They rigged up a cable
> But were completely unable
> To get anything other than jelly.

> A brilliant young lawyer in Taunton
> Conceived a desire t'be hauntin'.
> He cut off his legs
> And used them as pegs
> But his wife sent him packin' to Naunton.

The really confident could try clerihews instead of limericks.

Where Am I?

This is a simplified version of Botticelli (see p. 1). One person thinks of a place and an activity which could be done there. For example, he might think of being a guest on Desert Island Discs at Broadcasting House. And the female players might think of marrying Prince Edward in Westminster Abbey, or playing in the finals at Wimbledon. The other players attempt to guess the location and activity by asking questions which can only be answered by 'Yea' or 'Nay' (to ring the changes). No clues are allowed. Only twenty questions can be asked, or more if you put a mileage limit on them, say, forty in the next forty miles. The driver is umpire.

Headlines

The object here is to build amusing and attention-grabbing headlines of the sort favoured by the *Sun* and *News of the World*.

The first player begins a headline with a familiar word, such as vicar. The next adds a word before or after, so: Vicar Flees. It might continue as follows:

> Dirty Vicar Flees
> Dirty Vicar Flees Country
> Mother of Dirty Vicar Flees Country

After the headline has been round everyone once, the order of words can be changed and new words inserted anywhere:

> Country Vicar Flees Dirty Mother
> Mother of Three Flees Dirty Country Vicar

And so on. Conjunctions, tenses, numbers and other unimportant elements can be changed, as long as the basic units stay the same.

Associations

Also known as Chicken Egg Bacon, this must be played rapidly as it has no known point other than to build up as quickly as possible a long chain of associated words. Players who break the chain drop out, until there is only one triumphant person left.

A typical game might go like this:

> 'Wood.'
> 'Tree.'
> 'Frog.'
> 'Pond.'
> 'Cream.'
> 'Clotted.'
> 'Blood.'
> 'Stone.'
> 'What? How do you get stone from blood?'
> 'Because you can't get blood out of a stone, see?'
> 'OK, but it was close . . . Stone. Dead.'
> 'Umm . . . umm . . .'
> 'Out!'

And so on . . . and on . . . and on . . .

Pub Cricket

This game was invented by the historian Christopher Hibbert and his son Tom. It is no good for fast motorway driving – it needs an English road that wends its way through many a 'picturesque' village. You need to have two teams (of one or more a side), a coin and a scorepad.

Pub Cricket

The game is scored like a cricket match. The two teams pretend to be cricket sides (you can select people like Boycott, Bradman and Malcolm Marshall to play on your side and enter these names on your pad). The team that scores the most runs wins, just like in the real game. The scoring is based on pubs and pub signs and the number of legs contained therein. It's as easy as ABC.

First, toss to see who bats or fields. Then you must keep your eyes peeled for pubs and when you see one, shout very loudly. If the pub name has legs in it, the batting side scores runs. For example, the Bull and Bush: a bull has four legs, a bush none . . . 4 runs scored to the batsman. Or, the George, no doubt named after some King George or other, who had two legs, hence 2 runs scored to the batsman. But if you come across the Live and Let Live, a pub name that fails to feature any fauna in its title whatsoever . . . no legs equals no runs, which means a wicket for the bowler.

However, the score of the pub name may be overruled by the score of the pub sign if the legs on the latter differ – for example, if the pub is called the Queen's Head. A head, whether royal or not, has no legs directly attached to it, therefore this should be a wicket. However, the sign outside the Queen's Head may show Queen Elizabeth I sitting upon a throne with her legs *in situ*. Two portrayed legs equal 2 runs for the batsman. Or, the Orange Tree. A tree has no legs; however, the sign may show a tree with a bird sitting among the foliage. A bird has two legs, so 2 runs. It should be noted that the pub name can never be nullified to the bowler's advantage. For example, a pub called the Jolly Farmer counts for 2 runs (as a jolly farmer tends to have two legs) even if the sign is a painting of a bale of hay or something equally legless. The maximum amount of runs that can be scored upon a single stroke is 16. The Fox and Hounds *always* scores 12 (4 for the fox and 8 for the two hounds), unless the sign depicts masses of hounds, in which case the batsman can bump the score up to the maximum of 16. The Coach and Horses *always* scores 16. The players must assume that the coach is drawn by four horses, as was the norm. If the sign shows a coach being drawn by two horses this doesn't matter.

These are the Hibbert rules and must be obeyed.

Example

You are motoring through Gloucestershire and you pass . . .

The King's Arms (no sign) – wicket – score 0 for 1.

The Pig and Whistle (the sign shows a pig and a whistle) – 4 runs – score 4 for 1.

The Hedge and Thicket (the sign shows a thicket with a *bird* in it) – 2 runs – score 6 for 1.

The Miller (the sign shows a windmill) – 2 runs – score 8 for 1.

The Windmill (the sign shows a windmill) – wicket – score 8 for 2.

The Coach and Horses – 16 runs – score 24 for 2.

The Goat and Compasses (the sign shows a herd of goats) – 16 runs – score 40 for 2 – the bowler is getting a bit cheesed off.

The Queen's Head (no sign) – wicket – score 40 for 5.

The Cheddar Cheese (the sign shows bit of cheese) – wicket – score 40 for 6.

The Ship (no sign) – wicket – score 40 for 7.

The Queen's Head (no sign) – wicket – score 40 for 8.

The Cheddar Cheese (the sign shows a bit of cheese) – wicket – score 40 for 9.

(By this time it may have become obvious to the batsmen that the driver, one of the bowlers, is clearly cheating by driving round and round in circles, but . . . too late!)

The Ship (no sign) – wicket – 40 *all out*!

CHAPTER 2

ACTING AND IMPROVISATION

No acting games are easy for the shy and retiring. Playing in teams helps to conceal inhibitions, but never bully anyone into these sorts of games. There is always a need for an audience and non-players can have just as much fun as spectators or referees.

However, for show-offs and the uninhibited (or the tired and emotional) the games in this chapter give plenty of scope for their talents.

In the Manner of the Word

There are two versions of this game.

In the first, *one* person leaves the room. Those remaining choose an adverb – for example, madly, truly, deeply, sexily, brutally – which the absent person has to guess. When coming back into the room, the guesser can either ask questions which the others have to answer *in the manner of the word*, or ask any number of them to act out a situation, such as robbing a bank or cleaning your teeth, *in the manner of the word*.

In the second, *two* people leave the room to think of an adverb. Those remaining have to guess what it is by giving them situations to act *in the manner of the word*: for example, milking a cow, picking someone up, being refused a drink in a pub (in this version the situations should have two active parts).

Obviously the second is less inhibiting as you have someone with whom to share the agony. It also tends to be funnier, because you can tailor the situations to the

In the Manner of the Word

participants. Watching two aunts of a certain age and stature 'milking a cow timidly' was a hilarious sight.

Desire

Take a pack of ordinary playing cards and discard the royals and the aces, so that you are left with the cards from 2 to 10. Any number of people can play, but its success depends largely on having at least one active player who is not inhibited.

Two players sit together, facing the others in the room. They then pick a card each from the pack and have to act out the strength of their desire for each other, non-verbally, according to the numbers on their cards. The higher the card the stronger the desire. The rest of the party have to guess both levels.

As you can imagine, this game is rather more fun for the spectators. Desire is a game rife with embarrassing possibilities if you are not sure of who fancies whom. It can be a simple way of finding out, as when I innocently paired a girlfriend with one of my cousins, who was astonished at her enthusiasm when she was only holding a 3!

A canny games master may fix the cards to maximize embarrassment.

Four Options

This is best played by people who know each other well. Sit in a circle or round a table. Each player makes up a list of four people of the opposite sex to the person on his right and gives the list to that person. Of the four people on his list, each player has to decide, for instance, whom they would marry; whom they would have an affair with; whom they would betray; whom they would give a million pounds to.

Explanations for the choices should aim at the amusing rather than the literal. The questions can vary enormously, as can the names. Among acquaintances it might be best to stick to celebrities to avoid unnecessary embarrassment. Among friends, embarrassment is the name of the game. As in Desire, you can find out surprising things about them.

Who Am I?

This is not a game which necessarily has winners and losers. It is best played informally while washing up after dinner or while out for a walk.

Each person writes his name down on a piece of paper, which is folded and put into a hat. Everybody then picks one piece out of the hat and assumes that person's character. Given that all players know that someone in the room is being someone else in the room, guessing who is whom is not always very arduous. But the point (and the fun) is finding out people's perceptions of each other. Feelings can be hurt, but it isn't essential to the game's success to be mean.

Who Am I?

Of course, if you get your own name out of the hat, it can confuse everyone for hours. This happened once to me, and when I eventually admitted I was playing myself, the universal response was, 'But you're not *like* that!'

The Judge

All players except one, who becomes the Judge, form pairs and sit on the floor. You should form a pair with the person you're closest to, be it husband or wife, girlfriend or boyfriend. The Judge remains standing and starts the game by marching up and down the room in a manner befitting his station. He then suddenly turns to one partner of a pair and asks him or her a question. But it is the *other* partner of the pair who must answer. If the player questioned answers or the partner fails to, they are both out of the game.

The Game

As with so many of these acting games the aim is to cause as much embarrassment as possible. The Judge should make up questions that he knows the person to whom they are directed longs to answer and their partner patently doesn't, or vice versa. Speed is of the essence, and the game naturally works best among a group of people who have known each other for some time.

The Game

Again, there are two versions of The Game. Both involve players dividing into two teams. The first is more relaxed, a sort of spectator sport, with only one person in the spotlight; the second requires everyone to participate at the same time and tends towards chaos, but is all the better for that.

In the first, both teams secretly compile a list of book titles, film titles, proverbs, song titles, musicals, topical or historical events, tube stations or whatever. Team One then gives a member of Team Two a title to act out non-verbally to his own team-mates, who have to guess the answer, while Team One looks on and sniggers. When that round is over, the teams reverse roles. And so it goes on until both lists are finished.

The advantage of this version is that lists can be tailored to bring out the best or worst in individual members of the opposing team, or simply to – yes! – embarrass them!

In the second version there are two teams and one quiz-master who compiles the list. One person from each team is given the *same* title simultaneously by the quiz-master. They then return to their respective teams and act it out to their team-mates. The person who guesses correctly goes to the quiz-master to get the next title, and so on. The team which completes the list of titles first, wins.

Both teams are in the same room, so they should be far enough apart not to overhear each other's attempts to guess.

As this is a race, the pressure is on to perform quickly and appropriately. The quiz-master should keep a careful eye on both teams, especially watching for one team eavesdropping on the other, perhaps more talented group. Played this way, The Game gets very exciting, and noisy, as members of both teams shout, exhort, cajole, abuse and mock their actors. It can also be horrendously humiliating when you've taken five minutes on one seemingly simple word, and your entire team is watching (illicitly) the other actor.

For both versions there are various conventions to indicate whether what is being acted is a film title, book title, play, etc. These take the form of sign language, such as: opening and closing your palms to signify a book; drawing the rough shape of a proscenium arch of a theatre in the air with your fingers for a play; pulling sound (as it were) from your open mouth for an opera musical or song; making quotation marks in the air for a proverb; and anachronistically rolling the camera for a film. When stuck, as with topical events, it is just permissible to say *very* quickly, 'It's a topical event', and you can make up your own for tube stations.

Yet more conventions govern how you let the others know how many words there are in the phrase (by holding up that number of fingers in the air); which of the words

Symbols of The Game

you are acting at any point (for example, if you are acting out the fourth word, you indicate the fourth finger); how many syllables the word has (by laying the corresponding number of fingers across forearm); if the word or syllable rhymes with or sounds like something easier to act (by pulling the ear lobe). Little words, such as 'of', 'in', 'the', 'to', are indicated by holding up your thumb and forefinger slightly apart. If you are brave enough to act the whole thing out in one go, you draw a circle in the air with both hands. This doesn't always work: one of the more exuberant and daring renderings of *The Return of the Native* involved a stately lady of generous proportions leaving the room and tearing back into it while silently indicating with hand and mouth the noise of a Red Indian on the warpath. This was greeted with stony silence and blank stares. Her disappointment was profound.

Your team mates are allowed to shout out questions, but you can only nod or shake your head in response. *There must be no talking, whispering or even mouthing between actor and team.*

23

Here are some of the worst things I have had to either act myself or watch others go through torture over: the Defenestration of Prague, Beef Wellington, *Catholics* (as in the novel by Brian Moore), the Treaty of Maastricht, *By Grand Central Station I Sat Down and Wept*, *The World According to Garp*, *Oscar and Lucinda*, *Illywhacker* (almost any Peter Carey novel, in fact). You may be thinking, 'Oh, that's *easy*', but let me assure you they often look easier on paper.

Charades

Speech, clothes and props can be used in this, one of the oldest of parlour games.

Again, two teams are formed. Each one chooses its own two- or three-syllable word, which is then acted out to the other team, syllable by syllable, and finally the word itself. For example, 'nightingale' could be split into 'night', 'in', and 'gale'. Members of the team act out playlets, each containing the relevant syllable-word, the last playlet being the whole word. The knack is to disguise each syllable cunningly, or to 'bury' it in other words. For instance, 'night' might be used as 'knight'.

Once it was very popular in drawing-rooms up and down the country; now it is very much less so and is not a patch on the 'games of embarrassment' (see The Game p. 21, Desire, p. 18, In the Manner of the Word, p. 17).

Nebuchadnezzar

Here is another team game, which is a cross between Charades and The Game (see p. 21).

Both teams think of a famous person, one team then acting out to the other the name, letter, by letter using the initial letter of another famous name. For instance, Brahms might be mimed thus:

B – a deaf composer (Beethoven)
R – a disagreeable dwarf (Rumplestiltskin)

A – a pop group (Abba)
H – a mustachioed dictator (Hitler)
M – a cartoon mouse (Mickey)
S – Hamlet, Macbeth, etc. (Shakespeare)

In the unlikely event that the other team has not guessed the name of your original famous person by the end of this process, you and/or your team act out the *whole* name. The teams then swap.

The braver or more exhibitionist members of a team might like 'to do their own thing', but the entire team can join in and therefore this is often a more enjoyable bet for the shy than other acting games.

Jobs for the Boys

A sexist and totally inappropriate title for this hugely enjoyable game, which can produce inspired performances from the most uninhibited. But it is enormous fun for everyone else as well.

Each person thinks up a job and acts it out to the assembled company. Choosing Managing Director of A.N. Company is not going to make your life too easy or raise that many laughs. On the other hand, if your one-legged uncle is game enough to impersonate a ballerina or a gymnast, all the better. A popular choice of profession is that of rock guitarist (among men, inevitably), which may seem too obvious. However, as performed by a slightly podgy middle-aged banker, it can be extraordinarily funny.

Should you not want to rely on individuals choosing unfitting jobs for themselves, organize it as for The Game (see p. 21), with teams and an umpire with a list.

Smoke Signals

So-called, I can only imagine, because it involves the silent passing of information from one person to another, this could be Chinese Whispers without the verbal.

The party divides into two teams, one of which leaves the room. The team remaining decides upon a situation, one which requires a fair bit of acting, and calls in one member of the other team. The situation is acted out to him (by one person); he then calls in the next member of his team and tries to act out the same information to him. This continues until the last member, whose horrendous responsibility it is to guess what on earth is being acted out. By this time, of course, it will have undoubtedly departed somewhat from the original mime. The teams then reverse roles.

Possible situations could include:

> Receiving an emergency call, driving the ambulance, picking up the patient and returning to the hospital.
> Driving to the supermarket to go shopping, returning and unpacking the groceries.
> Morning ablutions and leaving for work.
> Cooking an omelette (or breakfast, or whatever).
> Presenting *Blue Peter*.
> Loafing around at work, having a row with your boss, getting sacked, getting drunk, going home to a furious partner.

Auditions

This is much enjoyed by show-offs and the shameless. One person, chosen by mutual consent (it is courteous to give it to someone who really loathes acting), conducts the auditions, deciding in the first instance whether the crowd will be speaking, miming, dancing, singing, or whatever. The auditioner then instructs the aspiring actors to perform in turn a range of emotions, which he shouts out one after another: fear, loathing, adoration, envy, anger, soppiness might be the sort of thing.

This does not really have winners, although it can be fiercely competitive. It should ideally be played for laughs.

CHAPTER 3

QUICK THINKING

Although some of these could be played in a car or on that old 3.45 to Edinburgh, just as Botticelli (see p. 1) can be played sitting round the fire, most of them are better suited to the comforts of home – curtains drawn against the wintry afternoon, bottles of plonk and beer to hand, and minds as alert as possible in the circumstances.

Of course, they will usually have to compete with the television, but sometimes there really isn't anything worth watching, and these games can be vastly more amusing.

Analogies

This is a far more difficult game to play correctly than it seems (and also more dangerous, as offence not meant can be easily taken).

One player thinks of a famous person or a person known to all those participating. The other players then try to guess the identity by asking him to describe the person he has chosen in terms of analogies. For example, if asked, 'What sort of building is he or she?', the answer could be anything from a town hall, to a 1930s' semi, to a castle in Spain. Analagous categories can be: modes of transport, animals, food, drinks, smells, weather, liquids, machines (industrial or domestic), flowers, books, furniture, etc.

Do not fall into the common trap of confusing what the person *likes* with what you *think* they are like. For example, someone who loves champagne is really more like fizzy lemonade (at least you think he is). And this is where the offence-not-meant-but-easily-taken occurs. I remember one friend describing another as a wheelbarrow, a perceived

Analogies

slight that has not been forgotten over many intervening years. One another occasion, two men took it in turns to insult each other, perhaps getting years of resentment off their respective chests, by likening each other to dirty bathwater and over-cooked spaghetti. The tension was tangible and only dissolved by everybody else's merriment. I was guilty of inflicting the unkind cut myself when I described a friend as a labrador. His humour got worse after the game when I admitted I had rejected poodle in favour of labrador. His wife joined in then . . .

For such reasons it is probably safer to use absent friends, or politicians, actresses and the like, who are fair game. With the latter there is also less likelihood of confusing what they like with what you think they are like, since you don't know them. But present friends make the best sport.

The Hat Game

Any amount of people, paired off, all think of two things each – book titles, film titles, film stars, pop stars, authors, proverbs, painters, expressions, etc. – which they write down on two scraps of paper. These are folded and thrown into a receptacle, such as a hat or saucepan. There should be twice as many bits of paper as people.

Now the game begins. One of a pair picks out a piece of paper and has one minute in which to describe to his partner what is written on it *without* using any of the key words in the title, or whatever, or any proper names, such as countries, towns, people's names.

For example, if you were describing *Gone With the Wind*, you might start thus: 'It's a four-word film title, a long film, about a headstrong Southern belle, her love affairs, set in a civil war (*not* the American civil war), and its most famous line is "Frankly my dear, I don't give a damn."' If your partner is still looking blank, then you've picked a right duffer, but you must persevere. When describing the content of a book or film doesn't work, you can describe the actual words: 'The last word is something that blows in the trees, and the first is the past participle of a general moving verb . . .' And your partner cries, 'I know, "Went with the Wind"!' Then you despair.

The trick is to keep talking at all costs, while your partner asks questions over the top of you, to which you quickly say 'Yes' or 'No', and then get on with describing.

The quicker your partner guesses the answer the better, as you then get to pick another piece, and so on until your time is up. The next pair then takes its turn. When all pairs have had one go, if there are any pieces of paper left in the saucepan, the first pair starts again but reverses roles. The winning pair is that with the most bits of paper.

This is a very fast-moving and exhilarating game, and an excellent exercise in succinct and precise description. Wafflers usually lose. So do those who are suddenly and inexplicably silenced by the requirement to speak. I once played with two friends, neither of them shrinking violets in normal conversation, who failed to win a single scrap of paper, as each was reduced to a kind of stuttering, mumbling wreck when it came to their turns. How the rest of us did laugh!

Buzz, Fizz and *Buzz-Fizz*

Are you feeling numerate? Sitting comfortably? In a rough circle? Now you can begin.

One player calls out, 'One', the next, 'Two', the next, 'Three', and so on. As soon as the number five or any multiple of five is reached, the player must say 'Buzz' instead of the number. If a number contains a five, but is not a multiple of it, only part of it is replaced by 'Buzz': for example, fifty-one (if you get that far) would be 'Buzz-one'. If a player forgets to say 'Buzz' or hesitates too long he drops out. The last in the game wins.

Fizz is exactly the same using sevens or multiples thereof. Most fiendish of all, and possibly only for mathematicians, is Buzz-Fizz, which combines fives and sevens and multiples of each.

Concentration is essential as the game should be played at high speed and it is all too easy to forget that thirty-five, for instance, is a 'Buzz' number, 'Fizz' number and a 'Buzz-Fizz' number. Pointless it may be, but it is quite simply one of the best games of this kind.

No, No

The simple objective here is to keep a chain of rhyming words going as long as possible. Someone thinks of a word which is easy to rhyme, such as goal. He then 'defines' it briefly, but he's really defining another word which rhymes with the first, and it is this second word the next player must figure out. He then announces that and defines a third word that rhymes with the first two. Each player has thirty seconds in which to figure out the defined word and think up another which rhymes. If he can't, that's it – he's out.

Example

Player One: A goal is something that lives in tunnels underground.

Player Two: No, no, you mean *mole*, which I burn in my fire.

Player Three: No, no, you mean *coal*, which Motown made popular.

Player Four: No, no, you mean *soul*, which you eat your cornflakes out of.

Player Five: No, no, you mean *bowl*, which you join a queue for.

Player One: No, no, you mean *dole*, which is sometimes difficult to get out of.

Player Two: No, no, you mean *hole*, which is a small rodent.

Player Three: No, no you mean *vole*, which you vault with.

And so on.

How Do You Like It?

This is a game of innuendo which can be made very funny depending on the wit and speed of players' reponses. One person leaves the room while the others think of a word.

When he returns he attempts to guess the word by asking everyone in turn the questions, 'How do you like it?', 'When do you like it?', and finally, 'Where do you like it?' The answers must be relevant, with subtly hidden clues. At any stage of the game the questioner can make a guess, and the person who lets the cat out of the bag takes the next turn.

In this example, I have chosen 'meat' as the word.

> *'How do you like it?'*
> Player One: Extracted.
> Player Two: Strong.
> Player Three: Blue.
> Player Four: Synthetic.

> *'When do you like it?'*
> Player One: On Sundays.
> Player Two: All the time.
> Player Three: For tea.
> Player Four: Never.

> *'Where do you like it?'*
> Player One: In my mouth.
> Player Two: In restaurants.
> Player Three: On my plate.
> Player Four: On an animal.

(Player Four is obviously some kind of veggie.)

I Have Never . . .

This is another of those games which is easy to misunderstand, as you will see.

Any amount of players can participate, the winner being he who has never done the most things, which doesn't on the face of it make much sense. But all will become clear.

Each person in turn announces that he has never done something which he is pretty sure that everyone else *will* have done. For instance: 'I have never eaten a grapefruit', 'I have never stayed a night in Scotland', 'I have never been to a pop concert', 'I have never passed an exam' (if this were true you probably wouldn't be playing this game – you'd be too busy running the country), 'I have never dived off a diving-board', 'I have never reread a book', are all the sort of things that most people can be expected to have done. However, if anybody else has also not done what you haven't done, you lose one of your three lives.

Why a lot of people lose all three lives rather rapidly is because they somehow confuse things that people are *likely* to have done with things which it is highly unlikely anyone in the room has done, like going to the moon, or meeting the Queen.

Pooh-sticks Banana

This is one of those deceptively simple games played to a tapped-out rhythm, which usually dissolves in chaotic hilarity. Two teams of up to four people each sit on opposite sides of a table. One member of one team is chosen to 'serve' a word, which he does by catching the eye of a member of the opposing team. As soon as the word is served, everyone starts tapping the table in unison, keeping a steady, but menacing beat. The 'return' word has to be made before the fourth beat, while eyeballing one of the other team, and has to either rhyme with or begin with the same letter as the 'served' word.

Sounds pretty simple, eh? But any word that begins with P must immediately be answered by 'Pooh-sticks', which in turn must be followed by 'Banana'. After 'Banana', any new word can be chosen. The game is scored as in tennis, i.e. 15-love, etc.

A rally might go as follows:

Cake	Bake
Bottom	Bun
Sun	Pun

Pooh-sticks	Bananas
Gate	Pate
Rate ... no, no, Pooh-sticks	

(15-love)

	Slippery
Slope	Grope
Hope	Cope
Rope	Scope
Sugar	Spice
Slice	Rice
Ice	Nice
Lice	Mice
Thrice	Twice
Dice	er ... er ...

(15-all)

Beware of rhymes: an ever-lengthening list of them can act like headlights on a rabbit – your mind freezes, unable to think of the simplest word, while the beat goes on and on and on ... Time's up! Like Buzz–Fizz, this is addictive fun.

Sixty Seconds

Listeners of Radio 4, for which it was devised by Ian Messiter, will know this game as 'Just a Minute'. Played skilfully by the likes of Clement Freud, Derek Nimmo and the late Kenneth Williams, it is hilariously and ingeniously funny. It can be an excellent parlour game, at which even ordinary mortals can shine.

One person, acting as games master or referee, armed with a stopwatch or a watch with a second hand, chooses a subject (one word or a short phrase) on which the other players have to expound for a minute. No repetition (except the subject word or phrase), hesitation or deviation is allowed. Other players can challenge the speaker on any of these. A person who makes a successful challenge takes the platform for however long is remaining of the minute, and the original speaker loses a point. An unsuccessful challenger loses a point, and the speaker continues and gains a point. Whoever is speaking when the full minute is up gets two points.

Anything will do as a subject: a word or phrase which has more than one application, such as bowls or wild birds, gives more scope, but absolutely anything will serve. Lack of knowledge is not necessarily a disadvantage.

The secrets of success are not to speak too fast (the faster you speak the more likely you are to repeat words and to hesitate), and not to wander off the subject while still exploring every possible related aspect of it. If, for instance, the subject were sailing, and you had an amusing anecdote about your attempts to master a dinghy, by all means tell it – but remember to return to the subject before you're accused of deviation.

Echoes

One person volunteers, or is coerced, to compile a list of definitions and the other players have to find two words which fit, and which also rhyme with or 'echo' each other. For example, the games master might call out 'Jolly baby's knicker', and a quick-witted player might answer 'Happy Nappy!' In the unlikely event that someone were to come up with 'Hyper Diaper', an argument would ensue – the games master's decision has to be final.

This must be played fast for maximum comic effect, either with players answering individually, or in teams if preferred. Here are some suggested clues and answers:

Oddity from Athens	Greek freak
Foolish goat	Silly billy
Broke Napoléon	Stony Boney
Oddity among holy men	Quaint saint
Inebriated man of the cloth	Drunk monk
Wicked parent	Bad dad
Gigantic fruit	Big fig
Amusing bride of Christ	Fun nun
Apologetic juggernaut	Sorry lorry
Malodorous tube	Smelly telly
Herbaceous influence	Flower power
Skinny royal	Lean queen
Suspicious statesman	Sinister minister
Mediterranean stud	Italian stallion

Naming Names

Another noisy, hand-clapping and table-thumping game which sweeps everyone up in its excitment. A rhythm is set up – *clap clap, bang bang* – and a nominated leader shouts out a category. For example:

Clap clap, bang bang
Leader: Names of . . .
Clap clap, bang bang
Leader (on the bang): Comedians.
Clap clap, bang bang
Player One: Charlie Chaplin.
Clap clap, bang bang
Player Two: Buster Keaton.
Clap clap, bang bang
Player Three: Tommy Cooper.
Clap clap, bang bang
Player Four: The Marx Brothers.
Clap clap, bang bang
And so on.

Players may have three lives, losing them for failure to come up with a name or for missing the beat. The leader changes when a category runs out of steam – which occurs extraordinarily quickly, even with large and easy categories, such as dog breeds. It's something to do with the insistent rhythm – your brain simply seizes up and panic sets in. Some suggested categories are: fat men, guitarists, painters, famous lovers – almost anything, depending on the company.

Going Blank

Going Blank is a game which is likely to make bullies of the mildest of mousy people, and in which speed is of the essence. One person is elected 'Inquisitor', and he thinks up and announces three categories, say film stars, French towns, and flowers. Standing in the middle of the room, he points aggressively and randomly at any one of the other players, and shouts out one of the categories. The person so attacked must quickly come up with an answer. The Inquisitor might swiftly jab his finger at another player, or he might stay with the same victim, shouting out another category or demanding another answer in the same category. For example:

> Inquisitor: Flower!
> Player One: Peony.
> Inquisitor: Flower!
> Player Two: Daisy.
> Inquisitor: French town!
> Player One: Rouen.
> Inquisitor: Film star!
> Player Three: Marilyn Monroe.
> Inquisitor: Film star!
> Player Three: Charlton Heston.
> Inquisitor: Film star!
> Player Three: Oh, for God's sake . . .
> Inquisitor: Out, out, out!

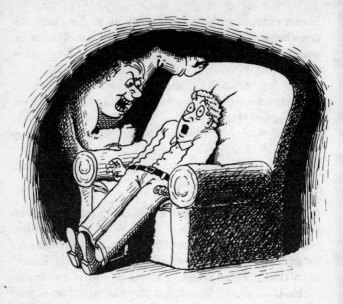

Going Blank

While demanding rapid successive answers in the same category from one individual is a sure-fire method of terrorizing the player to the point of departure from the game, it is pretty mean and the Inquisitor is only allowed to repeat the same category on the same person three times in a row.

I Accuse

One person is elected umpire and leaves the room with pencil and paper. One by one the other players go to him and give him the name of a famous person, be it an opera singer, a politician, a football player or golfer, a fictional character or whatever. A typical list might consist of the Archbishop of Canterbury, Anna Ford, Nick Faldo, Lester Piggot, Mick Jagger, Desperate Dan, Mrs Malaprop and Mrs Thatcher. When everyone has given a name, the umpire returns to the room and reads out the list twice. He then chooses who starts the game, and this person turns to whoever he thinks is most likely to have given a particular name, saying:

> Player One: I accuse you, Sarah, of being Mrs Malaprop.
>
> Player Two: No, but I accuse Nick of being the Archbishop of Canterbury.
>
> (You do not have to accuse the person who accused you.)

A person correctly accused drops out, and the accuser continues on to another person.

This is another of those bluff and double-bluff games. Therefore, if you are known to be an expert on football, either choose the name of a ballet dancer – or go for the double-bluff and choose a footballer, hoping that no one will believe you could be so obvious. It is best played among people who know each other a bit, but it also works as a warm-up for the horrible games which might follow as you get to know each other better.

CHAPTER 4

PENCIL AND PAPER

You may yawn at the thought of pencil and paper games, having outgrown them at fifteen. And you may have. But you grow *into* them again, any time after sixteen. Some of these games actually require a few working, or at least sober, brain cells; but most can be played post-prandially (some even benefit from it).

However, the most conducive setting for a round of anything from Battleships to Short Stories is a train journey. You are confined for possibly hours (plus delays), you are supplied with a table, and refreshments are available if needed.

Playing games on trains also guards against conversation with too many of those 'strangers who are just friends you haven't met yet'. Or it can help to sort this relatively rare breed from the strangers who you fervently hope will stay just that.

Categories

For this old favourite you give all the players the same long list of different categories. They should be as varied as possible. For example:

Parts of the body
Seven-letter words
Biblical characters
Words containing the letter Q
Musical terms
Battles
Characters from Dickens and Shakespeare
Bodies of water

Cathedral cities
European countries
American cities
Breeds of dogs
Monetary units
Furniture and furnishings
Dances
Names of sciences

The players are then given a letter of the alphabet, chosen at random, and have ten minutes in which to write down as many names as possible in each category beginning with the chosen letter. Obviously, the player with the most wins.

Disputed words are put to a majority vote. No score is given for a challenged word for which the writer cannot supply any backup information. Names of people means surname, not first name or title. Foreign names (of cities, etc.) only count in their anglicized form; for example, if you were searching for famous buildings and streets beginning with T, the *Tour Eiffel* would not count.

Concentration is vital, and easily lost. I once amassed an astonishing seventy names of famous people whose names began with H. My competitors were duly impressed . . . until I read my list out. Half-way through, the initial letter of the names had uncannily changed to W. Needless to say, I was disqualified.

Battleships

Like The Game (see p. 21), this has been played by generations of games players, often under other names, such as Jutland.

Two players take two pieces of paper each, on each of which they draw a ten-by-ten grid, numbered down the left-hand side, 1–10, and lettered across the top, A–J. One sheet is for the home fleet, the other is left blank to mark the enemy fleet's position. Each player's fleet consists of

Battleships

one battleship (made up of four squares), two cruisers (three squares each), three destroyers (two squares each) and four submarines (one square each). The squares that make up each ship must touch each other horizontally, vertically or diagonally. No two ships can touch each other by so much as a corner.

Each player marks up his home-fleet grid, using B for battleship, etc. In attempting to obliterate each other's fleet, each player in turn calls out a grid combination, such as B–3, hoping to hit an occupied square. All direct hits must be *honestly* declared and the type of ship specified. Anything from 'Nothing', to '*Tant pis*', to 'Ha ha, you missed, you bastard!' will suffice for an empty square.

Keep a record of your own calls on your blank enemy-fleet grid, and of your opponent's calls on your home-fleet grid.

The number and type of ships can be varied, depending on how long you want the game to last. You can even, by mutual agreement, decide on 'specials', such as the *Titanic*. Usually sinking the 'special' finishes the game. This can go

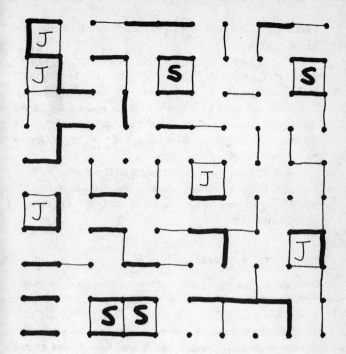

Boxes

wrong. I was once on a long train journey with a friend, who insisted that we had a 'special' *Belgrano* square. It was agreed between us that whoever hit the other's *Belgrano* first would win. I hit his on my first call, and the train hadn't even left the station. I think we played Noughts and Crosses after that.

Boxes

Mark out a piece of paper with a grid of dots, containing the same number of dots on each line vertically and horizontally. The two players then take it in turns to draw a line between *any* two dots in an attempt to form a square. Each player should have a different coloured pen. The player who makes a square marks it with his initial, and then may add one further line.

It should go without saying that each player is trying to prevent his opponent from completing a square. Strategy comes into play as the game progresses, and it gets increasingly difficult to draw a line without leaving a square for his opponent to complete. Then it is a question of damage limitation, i.e. drawing a line that will lead to the fewest number of completed squares.

It should also go without saying that the person with the most squares wins. Train journeys, plane journeys, any old sort of journey will be made less tedious by this surprisingly competitive game.

First Letters

This can be played by any amount of people. Each player calls out letters in turn, up to about fifteen, which are noted down in order by all players. Then the players have to concoct a sentence, the words of which must begin with the letters already agreed upon. A time limit of one minute is standard. For example:

L S P U M G R N W

This came out variously as:

> Lovely Scrumptious Percy Undressed Mrs Crabtree Ruinously Near Windsor.

> Let's Say Paul Undermined Matthew's Crass Retort Not Wittily.

> Lavinia Saw Peter Urinating Massively, Consciously Revolting Nearby Women.

After all the sentences are read aloud, everyone disagrees about which is the funniest. However, a useful yardstick with which to settle disputes is the volume of laughter generated, especially among other passengers (if on a train).

Stairway

A letter is chosen and the players are then given a set amount of time to build up as long a list as possible of words beginning with that letter: two letters long, then three, four, etc. For example:

D
DO
DON
DUMB
DEALS
DARKLY
DOLPHIN
DREADFUL
DUPLICATE
DESIGNATED

Go as far as your vocabulary or the train will take you in the available time.

Alphabet Race

This is a paper and pencil version of *Scrabble*. Each player lists the letters of the alphabet on his own piece of paper. A third piece of paper is placed between the two players and is the board. The first player writes down a word on the board and crosses those letters off his own list; the next player continues by adding a word to the board and crossing those off his list. You do not cross off your opponent's letters.

Say the first player used the word DAMN and the next MOURN, the board would look like this:

D A M N
    O
    U
    R
    N

So the second player would cross O, U, R and N off his list. And so it goes on, until one player has used up his alphabet. If a player gets stuck he can say 'Pass' and miss a turn.

Short Stories

This game is far more difficult than it seems. Everybody involved writes down the longest sentence they can only using words of three letters or less. You have two minutes. For example:

> I fed my dog and let her go out to see the cat but she sat on her bum and did not try to run to the cat so I got out my gun and I hit her and she was ded.

As you see, this can get very silly, and words really should be correctly spelt. An even harder version is to use only three-letter words (no more, no less). Hav fun!

The Dictionary Game

This is a parlour version of the now famous television show *Call My Bluff*. It is played in almost exactly the same way, except that you have to make up your own false definitions and you might never be as funny as Frank Muir et al.

A good dictionary is essential, so trains aren't always the ideal place to play. Players form two teams. One team picks an obscure word from the dictionary. One member of the team takes the real definition of the word, while the others invent convincing false definitions of it. They then present both real and false definitions to the opposing team, which has to determine the right one.

Specialized knowledge of practically anything comes in extremely useful. For instance, a person who knew a lot about horses might convincingly define 'quassia' as a special bridle used for training horses in dressage. It is, in fact, a South American tree.

Pictures

This is a visual and less hectic version of The Game (see p. 21). Anyone who ever received as a child, or has written as an adult, one of those pictorial letters will understand the principle immediately. However, here you cannot use any letters of the alphabet at all.

There are two teams, one of which gives a member of the other a book or film title, a proverb or whatever to draw for his team. The object is to guess what the drawing depicts as quickly as possible. When the answer has been guessed correctly, the teams reverse roles.

As in the acting version, symbols are used to indicate a book, a play, a film, etc. Simply draw the appropriate symbol – an arch for a play, a camera or film can for a film – it may sound too technical but you don't have to be van Gogh. The number of words is indicated by Morse code dashes, syllables by dots. For 'This sounds like . . .', draw an ear.

This can be even harder than its older brother. Obviously some titles lend themselves immediately to illustration, such as *Three Men in a Boat*. But others defy literal depiction, requiring you to go down lengthy side-roads, via rhymes and other diversions – try *Casablanca* or *Nicholas Nickleby*.

Transformation

This is more difficult than it might seem. The same pairs of words are given to every player, who then tries to convert one word to the other in the least number of steps, changing only one letter at a time. For instance, given 'dog' to 'cat', 'wolf' to 'lamb', etc., you might do:

DOG, COG, COT, CAT.
WOLF, WOLD, SOLD, SOLE, SOME, SAME,
LAME, LAMB
HEAT, HEAD, HELD, HOLD, COLD
BOOT, BOOK, COOK, COCK, SOCK

This is a useful game for short hops, such as Paddington to Reading, or York to Scarborough.

Find the Bird, Animal, Tree or Flower

Players devise sentences which contain the names of any of the above cleverly hidden in them. For example:

It was a shalloW RENdering of such a great work. (WREN)

It was difficult TO ADhere to the rules. (TOAD)

The yellow keLIM Emphasised the poppy-red walls. (LIME)

I can tyPE ONYour machine if you show me how. (PEONY)

Bridge the Word

Each player draws six lines across his piece of paper. A six-letter word chosen by mutual agreement is written down the left-hand side of the paper, with each letter beginning a line. The same word is written backwards down the right-hand side. For example:

D	Y
O	E
N	K
K	N
E	O
Y	D

Now you have to bridge the first and last letters, to create a word using as many letters as possible. The person with the longest words wins. For instance:

DepilatorY
OrganizE
NightsticK
KitcheN
EspressO
YuppifieD

beats

DailY
OrE
NicK
KiN
EgO
YarD

obviously.

Anagrams

Anagrams is an ideal game for those subdued, rainy afternoons: arguments about it are impossible; it requires a certain degree of concentration, but still allows for the occasional wry aside, and quiet wit.

It can be played in teams or individually. One person draws up the usual list of categories (such as flowers, parts of the body, planets and stars, pop stars, films), each containing up to six anagramized words. He then spells aloud each anagram, which the players take down and try to solve in an alloted time, say five minutes per category, or less if the categories are short. The individual player or team who solves most in the time wins and compiles the next list.

Here are some categories and anagrams to start you off:

49

Politicians

Roll Me	Mellor
Char Hett	Thatcher
Shiten Eel	Heseltine
Teckbet	Beckett
Nod Wash	Ashdown
Motley Tob	Bottomley

Films

Zluu	Zulu
Alcancabas	Casablanca
Hindh Matter	The Third Man
Dogger Flin	Goldfinger
Hubren	Ben Hur
Primo Snappy	Mary Poppins

Novelists – Contemporary

Senrab	Barnes
Tradlanc	Cartland
Her Car	Archer
All Drab	Ballard
Barbled	Drabble
Yakdroc	Ackroyd

Birds

Pro Wars	Sparrow
Pigame	Magpie
Niff Up	Puffin
Leage	Eagle
Log In Maf	Flamingo
But Lite	Blue Tit

Pop Singers and Groups

Dan O Man	Madonna
Pincer	Prince
Teeth Bales	The Beatles
Glass Trern	Stranglers
Six Set Slop	Sex Pistols
Rum Chap Roul	Procul Harum

Cars

Tug A Bit	Bugatti
Ban Tart	Trabant
Laurent	Renault
Lamerid	Daimler
Stir Bol	Bristol
Rand Lover	Land Rover

Hamlet

Inspired by a competition in the *New Statesman*, the objective here is deftly and succinctly to bring to an untimely end any work of fiction – opera, musical, poem, novel, film or drama.

Each person names a work of fiction which everyone writes down. At the end of five minutes each person reads out his lines which would have ensured those particular stories would never have been told. For example:

Waiting for Godot
Act I, Scene i   [*Enter* GODOT.]

Jane Eyre
Chapter One   When Mr Rochester told me that the madwoman in the attic was his wife, I left his employment.

Macbeth
Act I, Scene i
FIRST WITCH: All hail Macbeth, that shalt be king hereafter.
SECOND WITCH: Thou shalt murder the Thane of Cawdor, and the King.
THIRD WITCH: No man of woman born shall hurt thee.
FIRST WITCH: But Macduff, born by Caesarean, shalt murder thee.

Othello
Act I, Scene i
My Lord, I have mislaid that handkerchief you fondly
gave me.

Lord of the Flies
Chapter One   After a few hours on the island, the
boys were most relieved to see a
vessel approaching.

The Rime of the Ancient Mariner
It is an ancient mariner,
And he stoppeth none of three.

Blurbs

Another 'literary' game, Blurbs can be played competit-
ively or simply for amusement.

Each player takes two minutes to write the kind of
sensational blurb found on the backs of bestselling paper-
backs, but about a 'serious' work of fiction of their choice.
Players then each read out their own blurbs, the others
guessing the real title of the work described. The winner is
he who guesses the most correctly.

Alternatively, one person compiles a list of, say, up to
three titles which he reads out to the others, who then
write short and sensational blurbs. These are read out for
everybody's amusement. This version lasts longer and is
less competitive. In both cases, the aim is to be misleadingly
truthful. Here are a few examples:

Wuthering Heights

A beautiful wayward girl is torn between lust and ambition.
She loves her wild and darkly handsome man o'er the hills,
but knows that Steady Eddie will fulfil her passionate need
for the finest things in life.

Can she give up her rebel lover? Will he let her?

A Tale of Two Cities

A multi-stranded love story set in the turbulence of history. A man whose appetites have been his ruin is enchanted by a pure young beauty. His love for her is his redemption. But she loves another who is under the shadow of death. Can he make the ultimate sacrifice for love?

Heroism, romance and suspense combine to produce a fast-moving and unputdownable story of life among society's most powerful and beautiful people.

Pride & Prejudice

Greed! Snobbery! Loyalty! Love! Trust! Friendship! Marriage! Shame!

All the stuff of life is captured in this sensational tale of five sisters on the hunt for top-notch husbands. Will they find them? What obstacles lie in wait to bring them down? Who will make the best catch?

As their anxious mother looks on, we follow the ups and downs of fiction's favourite family!

Moby Dick

A rip-roaring tale of one man's quest for the ultimate prize! A story of vaunting ambition, of overweening pride, and of an all-consuming obsession.

In this epic adventure a man with nothing more than a glint in his eye, a spear in his hand and ice in his heart searches the seas for his mortal enemy – and his fanaticism leads to mayhem and carnage in a spectacular and catastrophic finale.

Telegrams

A game to keep you occupied at least from London to Birmingham. Pick a word at random from a newspaper or magazine, write it down and invent a telegram, each word of which begins with the letters of the chosen word in the right order. STOP can be used without an S being in the word. Allow a minute to complete the telegram. Thus, VENTURE might become:

VEGETARIAN ELEPHANT NEEDS
TURNIPS URGENTLY STOP RUMBLING
EXTREME
or
VILLAINOUS EDDIE NICKED STOP TELL
UNCLE REWARD ENORMOUS.

Last Names

In a similar vein to the above, each person is given the name of a famous person, historical, current or fictional (you can of course use mutual friends or foes). Players write a sentence appropriate to that person's character, each word beginning with the letters of the surname used in the correct order.

Sentences based on Mick Jagger or John Major might read:

Jumping Ageing Goer Gets Elephantiasis Rash.

Mediocre Administrator Junks Our Realm.

If you had a friend named Barrowclough, who also happened to be a hunting, wine-loving solicitor, a sentence might go:

Beefy And Rowdy Rider Owning Wine Cellar Legislates On Uncouth Gin Houses.

The Poetry Game

Don't be put off by the 'learned' sound of this game. You don't have either to have read a great deal of poetry or to excel at the composition of it – it's really a vaguely rhyming and scanning version of Consequences (see below).

Provide everyone with pencil and paper. Each person writes two lines of verse, either of his own invention or remembered, folds the paper over the first line, and passes it to the person on his left, who writes the third line. The game continues thus, each person receiving one visible line and writing one until a set length is reached – eight lines makes a decent poem. Each poem is then read out, it is hoped, to praise and applause.

Consequences

Nearly everybody has played this at some point, usually with indulgent grandparents or parents. In an 'adults only' game, it can often become more personal, ruder, and therefore – of course – funnier.

Consequences normally follows a set format, the most common of which is probably this one:

Male character
Female character
Where they met
What he did
What she did
What he said
What she said
The consequence was . . .
The world said . . .

Armed with pencil and paper, each person first writes the name of the male character, folds the paper to hide what he has written, and passes it on. Everyone then supplies each of the next categories, folding the paper every time, until the consequence, and the world's reaction to it, are reached. The stories are then read out to huge amusement. A few rounds usually suffice.

Picture Consequences

This is exactly as above, but you draw a picture of a 'creature'. It should be decided beforehand how much of the drawing can be completed at each stage: for example, head and neck only, then shoulders to elbows, etc. Each fold of the paper should leave just enough of the drawing visible so that the next person knows where to attach his bit. And it goes without saying that it is not necessary to stick to the human form, clothed or unclothed.

First Lines

Here is another literary-sounding game which doesn't require a First in English to enjoy. In fact, the scoring works against those who might occasionally recognize the first line of a novel.

Players take it in turns to be umpire and pick at random any book, from a novel to a travelogue, to a DIY manual. The umpire announces the title of the work and gives a brief description of it (taken from the fly-leaf or wherever). He writes down the real first line, and everybody else writes down what they imagine the first line to be. It is advisable to put a time limit of, say, one minute to prevent smart alecs from taking this too seriously.

When everyone has supplied their first lines, the umpire collects the papers and reads out their contents. He then reads them again, this time allowing votes to be cast for the most convincing line. The person who supplied the most voted-for line gets two points. Anybody guessing the real first line only gets one.

People who pride themselves on their appreciation of the many genres in English literature are said to take not

Picture Consequences

inconsiderable satisfaction in supplying lines that out-Hardy Hardy or are more Amis than Amis.

Since British Rail has yet to provide passengers with decent libraries, this one is best played at home.

CHAPTER 5

LATE NIGHT AND BOISTEROUS

People are often most enthusiastic about playing games when a good dinner and fine wines have smoothed away tensions. This is also a time when standing on one's dignity has become rather an effort, and the following games are perfectly suited to such a state of mind. None is dignified, some will make you look positively idiotic, others will get you blind drunk, but they are all worth trying.

Plum Plum Plum

Some would say this is really a children's game, but it is in fact much faster and often more fun without them. Adults, however, are best at it when suitably relaxed by a long dinner. When played under the right conditions, it would be hard to find a more universally enjoyed game.

It could hardly be simpler. Everybody finds somewhere to sit in a rough circle round the room, leaving a largish space in the middle. One person stands in the centre, while the others each announce the name of a fruit. The man-in-the-middle has to remember who is which fruit, or more accurately which seat is which fruit. This will become clearer.

He then spins around, without falling over, picks his fruit/person, and points at him while shouting 'Plum', for instance, *three times* before the person who is plum says it once. In the highly likely event of him failing, he moves on to another fruit/person. Should the man-in-the-middle *succeed* in this ludicrous, but extraordinarily difficult endeavour, he swaps places with 'plum', and so becomes 'plum'.

Plum Plum Plum

And so it goes on, the new man-in-the-middle trying to catch someone else out, and when successful taking on that fruit. Obviously, it becomes harder to remember where each fruit is as people change places, since one's instinct is to attach a face, rather than a chair, to a fruit.

Some people think it frightfully clever to choose such fruits as pomegranate, apricot, or pawpaw, hoping to sit tight throughout the game. However, an experienced man-in-the-middle will soon catch out such unsporting cads, and woe betide them when they are in the middle.

Plum Plum Plum gets extremely noisy and argumentative, as there are few rules to govern it, but many slightly devious tricks that can be employed by the man-in-the-middle. For instance, a favourite tactic is to turn quickly on the fruit who has just put you in the middle, before he has had time to sit down, pick up his drink and get acquainted with his new name. This is strictly not on. Other forbidden behaviour is to start saying a fruit before looking at your victim. Pointing is absolutely essential. The key element in the successful man-in-the-middle's strategy will always be surprise.

Animal Snap

Animal Snap is another game often demoted to children's parties, but which again can be far more amusing played by party-spirited adults.

As with ordinary Snap, a pack of cards is dealt (use two packs if necessary, even incomplete ones) to all the players, who choose and announce their animal noises. Thus, 'baa-baa', 'oink-oink', 'quack-quack', etc. (Honestly, this *is* a very funny game.) You then play Snap. But, instead of shouting out that tired old word when two cards match, you shout out the animal noise belonging to the player of the matching card, *not your own*. If a third party is very quick off the mark, he can win by shouting the animal noises belonging to the players of *both* the matching cards.

People have been known to get very excitable as the evening wears on, transported further than Bottom ever was when he grew the ass's head. A highly successful magazine publisher, who should have known better, suprised us all once by allowing his enthusiasm to carry him to unacceptable levels of boorishness. With victory in his sights, he leapt to his knees, elbowing all competition aside, eyes popping, and yelling, 'Bow-f*****g-wow!' He won.

Like Plum Plum Plum (see p. 59), this is a game which wins over even people so stuffy you could sit on them. However, a certain novelist comes to mind, whose stuffing was unimpressionable. While all around were bow-wowing, and baa-ing, and miaowing and oinking merrily, he sat stony-faced and superior. So be warned: there are those who just can't make animal noises.

Shop Snap

This is exactly as above, but instead of choosing an animal, each player chooses a kind of shop, such as fishmonger, haberdasher, butcher, etc. Department stores are *not* allowed.

When two matching cards are turned up, you have to

61

ask for something from your opponent's shop before he asks for something from yours. Under pressure, you are more than likely to ask for a pound of mackerel when you should be asking for three metres of velvet ribbon. Or you could be left making goldfish mouths while your opponent rattles off a list of everything your shop could possibly sell.

The following example of the heights of hysteria the game can reach comes from a description by the actress Maureen Lipman in her book *When's It Coming Out?*:

I know it sounds easy but I can assure you it's heinous. Not only can you not remember what shop they are but once you have remembered that it was a cake shop, the only word that comes out of your mouth at full decibels, for some reason, is 'Portrait! Portrait!' which you yell repeatedly, until the other person has finished ordering a pound and a half of whiting and some crabsticks from you. And you, it goes without saying, were the sex shop.

Moderately normal, mildmannered people who teach schoolchildren or floss bridgework turn into frothing imbeciles before your very eyes. Some go completely silent but for the regular opening and closing of their mouths. Some speak in tongues, saying 'gimp' or 'fallo fallo erk' in a higher and higher pitch until they faint and others physically grow in stature and point their fingers into the cornea of the person opposite bellowing, 'I want a large – large – largest biggest bargest large huge enormous great steaming big *wharrever it is you stock in your effing shop!*'

Are You There, Moriarty?

How this spectacularly brutal, violent and unsubtle game ever came to be named after Sherlock Holmes's deviously clever enemy is anyone's guess.

Two people are blindfolded and lie down facing each other. They hold each other's left hand, keeping their elbows on the floor. In their right hands they each hold a tightly rolled up newspaper. Player One asks Player Two, 'Are you there, Moriarty?', to which Player Two must reply, 'I am here.' Using his judgement as to where the voice came from, Player One attempts to thwack Player Two's head as hard as he can. If he succeeds, he's allowed another go, if he misses, Player Two tries to get his own back.

Obviously, the idea is to avoid a battering by quietly, Moriarty-like, moving your head *after* answering 'I am here' so that your opponent misses. Equally obviously, the hitter should take such tactics into account, as Holmes might have done. The referee, as well as ensuring that blindfold material is not transparent (it has been known!), retains the power to retire a hurt player early.

This game is nearly always more fun for the onlookers.

Cardinal Puff or *Colonel Bogey*

This is a game for hardened and foolhardy drinkers, which guarantees a head like a cannonball and a mouth like the inside of a chauffeur's glove the next morning, the penalty for making a mistake being to drink more and more. This is the one constant element of its many variations.

The object of the game is to drink a toast to Cardinal Puff or Colonel Bogey by performing a sequence of seemingly simple actions without hesitation or the slightest deviation. What follows is one fairly well-known version.

Participants sit round the table, each with a primed glass of wine or beer in front of him. (Other beverages can be used – whisky, vodka, etc. – but . . .) The first player begins by standing up and addressing the others with the words, 'I drink to the health of Cardinal Puff for the first time.' Having thus committed himself, he extends one finger of each hand and taps the top of the table, once with the left-hand finger and once with the right; he then taps the underneath of the table, once with the left-hand finger and once with the right-hand; his left leg with his left-hand finger, his right leg with his right-hand finger; his left chest with his left-hand finger and his right chest with his right finger. He then picks up the glass with his thumb and one finger, bows once to his companions, takes one sip and taps the glass once upon the table.

He then says, 'I drink to the health of Cardinal Puff Puff

Cardinal Puff or *Colonel Bogey*

for the second time.' He then repeats the whole sequence using two fingers and tapping twice at each stage. He picks up the glass with the thumb and two fingers, bows twice to his companions, takes two sips from the glass, and taps the glass twice on the table.

Then, he says (you guessed it!), 'I drink to the health of Cardinal Puff Puff Puff for the third and last time.' He repeats the sequence with three fingers, tapping thrice at each stage, picks up the glass with thumb and three fingers, bows three times, and takes three sips from the glass making sure to drain it on the third. He taps it *twice* on the table, turning it over on the third.

If he has done this to the complete satisfaction of his fellow toasters, who all the while have been sticking their tongues out at him, telling him jokes, making personal remarks in an attempt to make him falter, he can sit down and join them in undermining the next player's efforts. Remember, at the first hint of any mistake or hesitation, it's back to square one.

Oh dear, another drink.

Ruthless Truthless

Although not a drinking game *per se*, a few glasses may provide the bravado necessary to face the critical onslaught from one's so-called friends whose honesty is in turn brutalized by the same. In fact, the after-effects of this game may well last rather longer than those of Cardinal Puff. Weeks later you may suddenly wonder *why* Barrowclough said you were a nymphomaniac, or exactly what Sheila meant when she made that remark about your relationship with your mother. A game that should be treated with caution.

One person leaves the room. The others each write down a statement about the absentee, the list being given to him when called back. He then tries to identify who said what by asking indirect questions of each player, such as: 'When you said what you said did you know I was a virgin until I was twenty-five?' These types of question, limitless in number, need not necessarily be answered truthfully. Direct challenges to a player, such as, 'Sheila, did you say that my mother and I have a co-dependent relationship?' must be answered truthfully, but the player is only allowed as many challenges as there are other players.

The round finishes when all statements have been correctly attributed, or challenges have been used, or, in extreme cases, once the subject has been reduced to a shadow of himself, gibbering about loyalty and friendship.

Giants, Wizards, Elves

Really a full-bodied version of Scissors, Paper, Stone (see p. 3), this is said to be a favourite after-dinner pastime at Channel 4 conferences, when television executives of both sexes, normally known for their restraint and impassiveness, are to be heard shrieking, screaming, roaring and giggling.

Conferees divide into two teams and retreat to the opposite ends of the room. The teams then line up along their walls, facing each other. On a given signal, they advance down the room towards each other, and when about three paces apart everybody individually bellows out, 'Giant', 'Wizard' or 'Elf' at the person immediately opposite. Giants ball their fists and raise their arms, wizards stretch out their arms as if casting a spell, and elves crouch down and look elfin.

Giants capture wizards because they are bigger; wizards capture elves because they are cleverer; and elves get giants because they can run circles round them. Captives are taken back to enemy lines, and are press-ganged into service. The object is to capture the entire enemy team, but as you can imagine this takes a very long time, the noise level rises, hysteria takes over and games usually end in chaos.

Good Morning, Madam

Another Snap-type game best played without children, when it can be enjoyed to the full.

One or two packs of cards, depending on the number of players, is dealt. Taking turns, each player puts down a card on a central pile, the object being to win all the cards. The winning cards are Ace, King, Queen and Knave. When an Ace appears, everyone slams down the palm of their hand on top of it. First down wins, and shakes his throbbing hand. King: everyone executes a British Army salute – and quick about it. Knave: everyone executes a Heil Hitler salute, attempting not to poke anybody's eye out (no penalties for wounding). And Queen: everybody yells, 'Good morning, Madam', as loudly as possible. This is invariably followed by even louder yelling about who said it first.

People usually play this game late at night and well in their cups, with the result that neighbours are best avoided the next day. A banker friend of mine was once sharing a remote cottage with similarly upstanding pillars of the City. After a delicious dinner during which high finance and the state of the nation were discussed, the men who look after our money thought they'd have a quick round of Good Morning, Madam. Several hours later, the local constabulary arrived, concerned about some blood-curdling yells which had been reported by the farmer in the next valley. This is a typical example of the effect the game can have on bankers . . .

The Spanking Game

I was introduced to this sado-masochistic game by a quite extraordinarily glamorous model, whom one could hardly imagine enjoying it. But she did!

One person sits in a chair, while another kneels in front with his head buried in the other's lap. The rest of the party run around this tableau, taking turns to spank the bottom of the kneeler, who has to guess the identity of any one of the spankers. When a spanker is recognized, he kneels and chooses another player to take the chair. (The sitter's main function is to make sure the kneeler doesn't peep.)

The model's spank was barely more than a caress, but another in the party, a peculiarly scrubbed gentleman of military bearing, brought to bear the full force of his right arm. This made his spank easily identifiable, and one could only assume that he more than liked having his bottom smacked. He also always chose the model's lap in which to bury his face . . .

The Buttock Game

A splendidly silly game, only ever played when people's inhibitions have long been drowned, it is apparently very popular among certain 'fun-loving' members of the Royal Family.

A dish (silver is probably used at the Castle, but anything that makes a good clink will do) is placed on the floor at one end of the room. Each player takes turns to transport a coin – a five-pence piece is not recommended, for reasons that will become clear – the length of the room and deposit it in the receptacle provided, which must remain on the floor.

It sounds simple – but the coin has to be carried *clenched between the buttocks* (undressing is not necessary). This has the effect of radically altering the way people walk, and induces extraordinarily comical expressions of concentration, to the vast amusement of onlookers. If a winner is needed, it is the person who 'clinks' the coin into the dish most often – or the person who looks most risible as he clenches muscles he didn't know he had. To make it more difficult, try using a cup; to make it well nigh impossible, substitute an eggcup, for which a five-pence piece will be essential.

A variation is to divide the party into two teams and play it as a race. Two chairs are placed at the opposite end of the room to the receptacles, and an object such as a golf ball is put on each. The two teams line up behind the chairs and on the word 'Go', the first player from each team attempts to collect the golf ball between his buttocks (no hands allowed), carry it down to the receptacles and drop it in. If successful, he takes the ball back to the chair in his hand for the next player. If he drops it on the way, or misses the receptacle, he takes the ball back to the chair and starts again with his buttocks. Fiendishly difficult!

Strip Poker

This hardy perennial hardly needs explanation, and for some reason is despised by many games players. It seems to be regarded as Essex Man's and Girl's game. There certainly seems to be an age barrier, which is around twenty-five.

Natural modesty usually takes over thereafter, but some 'young adults' do seem to get thrills out of the possibility of being defrocked in public.

You simply play any kind of poker you want – high-low, five-card stud, seven-card flip, roll-over, or whatever – and bet in the usual way. The losing player(s) take off an item of clothing nominated by the winner. If you're like me, and simply hate this game, you will prepare beforehand by putting on extra layers. This could be construed as cheating, but for me it is the only possible way of playing. There always seems to be an exhibitionist who starts off practically naked.

Bang

This must be played *very* fast and with total concentration. It simply doesn't work if players continue their conversations about the state of the world or their friends' marriages.

The party is divided into two teams who sit opposite each other. Place a chair with a cushion on it at one end of the room equidistant to the teams. Each team writes the names of the individuals in the opposing team on scraps of paper. Team A starts by placing one of the scraps underneath the cushion on the chair and inviting members of the other team to choose who of their number is to sit on the chair. The aim is to *not* sit on your own name. If a player does so, Team A shouts, as loudly as possible, 'Bang', pointing imaginary guns if they are so inclined, and thus 'killing' that player. It is then Team B's turn to place a name under the cushion. If the name under the cushion does not correspond with the sitter, he returns unharmed to his team, and they place a new name under the cushion. And on it goes until one team has no live players left.

Any skill there is in this game is in the ability to outwit the opposing team. Devious players can make to lower their bottoms *very* slowly while scanning the opposing

Strip Poker

team for any signs of murderous intent. If he suspects he might be about to cop it by sitting on his own name, he can return to his team and send someone else. Poker-faces are a must. On each team there is always a natural victim (not necessarily a wimp – indeed, probably someone's best friend), who will be gunned for. So it is a question of bluff, double bluff, and triple bluff.

Cleat

The seemingly simple objective of this silly enterprise is to make one person laugh by asking him insinuating questions which he has to answer with one word that has been given to him beforehand.

Success depends on the suggestiveness of the 'answer-word', as well as on the questioners' powers of innuendo, which can undermine the responder's determination to keep a straight face. However, a skilled practitioner can ignore the *doubles entendres* time after time, while reducing the questioners to a state of helpless merriment.

A particular favourite as 'answer-word' is cleat, which happily lends itself to misinterpretation, and can seem killingly funny in answer to the most innocuous questions, such as: 'Where do you park your car?'

'Why, in my cleat . . .'

Sardines

You may think you are too old for this game, but it has its point if for no other reason than it affords a weary games player a bit of peace and quiet. There is nearly always a reluctant participant, and he or she should be made to hide first.

After he has gone to hide and he has been given ample time, the lights are turned out while the others scour the house in search of the original sardine. Whenever a player finds him, he joins him wherever he is – under a bed, or even in it, in the attic, in the coal cellar or a cupboard –

taking care not be seen by any of the others. The last person to discover the shoal's hidey-hole has to be the next sardine.

I once played a game of Sardines started purely to get rid of a particularly irksome member of our party. No one really wanted to play, except him. So we sent him off to hide, and got on with whatever we were doing. He must have sat in the cupboard for a good forty minutes before he rumbled the fact that no one was looking for him. We haven't seen him for years.

The Prince of Wales Has Lost His Hat

This is an incredibly complicated game both to explain and to play. The more sober you are the easier it is to master; on the other hand, you are only likely to consider playing it when half-seas over.

At least six players are needed to make it work well. Sitting round a table, each player is numbered clockwise, and the game proceeds as follows:

> Player One: The Prince of Wales has lost his hat and Number Three has found it.
> Player Three: No, sir. Not I, sir.
> Player One: Then who, sir?
> Player Three: Five, sir.
> Player Five: No, sir. Not I, sir.
> Player Three: Then who, sir?
> Player Five: Two, sir.
> Player Two: No, sir. Not I, sir.
> Player Five: Then who, sir?
> Player Two: One, sir.

This should be done as fast as possible. The first person to change the formula or fluff his lines is moved to the last chair round the table, in this case Number Six. If Number Two bungles, he moves to Six, Six moves to Five, Five to Four, and so on. In this instance only Number One would stay put.

All this moving around and changing numbers just serves to muddle further an already mind-boggling game.

I have never known this to be simple but, if you are an amazingly quick-witted (and sober) bunch, you might try this 'advanced' version, wherein the first four players are named John, Paul, George and Ringo, while the remaining players are numbered. For example:

> John: The Prince of Wales has lost his hat and Number Five has found it.
> Player Five: No, John. Not I, John.
> John: Then who, sir?
> Player Five: Ringo, John.
> Ringo: No, sir. Not I, sir.
> Player Five: Then who, Ringo?
> Ringo: Paul, sir.
> Paul: No, Ringo. Not I, Ringo.
> Ringo: Then who, Paul?
> Paul: Six, Ringo.
> Player Six: No, Paul. Not I, Paul.

As you can see, John and the other three are addressed by their names, while the numbered players are addressed as 'sir'. Fluffs and hesitations are dealt with as before. You might like to try a dry run at breakfast, when some minds are sharpish – provided you haven't played Cardinal Puff (see p. 63) the night before!

Noah's Ark

Noah's Ark is most definitely a late-night game, and is probably most effective after a round or two of Cardinal Puff (see p. 63), or as release from the rigours of trying to find the Prince of Wales's hat.

Write down the names of animals on pieces of paper, in pairs so that there are as many pairs of animals as there are pairs of people. The obvious way to divide the party up is according to gender, but it can also be done according to height or simply arbitrarily. The folded pieces of paper are put into two hats or whatever, one donkey or cat or chicken in each receptacle. One hat is given to each team, the members of which then pick out a piece of paper from it. From then on players may only talk in the noise of the animal they have picked.

Down on all fours, everybody attempts to find their mate by clucking, snorting, whinnying, barking, etc. Uproarious!

The Kissing Game

The ideal mood in which to play this is one of relaxed, expansive, unembarrassed friendliness. Don't attempt to join in if you are remotely shy.

One player is blindfolded and placed in the centre of the circle formed by the others. He spins around a few times before advancing towards the circle. On encountering a player, he has to kiss that person on the lips, with as much enthusiasm as can be mustered. This should alert him to the identity of the kissee, and if he guesses correctly they swap places. If he fails, he has to continue kissing unknown lips until he matches a pair with a name.

As you can imagine, this is a game which can on occasion lead to recriminations. 'How come, darling, you were able to identify *quite* so many lips?' 'Why did you have to kiss so-and-so for *quite* such a long time?' Or even, 'Why didn't you recognize my lips *once* all evening?'

The Taste Game

Perhaps familiar from children's parties, when it was played with nice-tasting drinks, this is a nastier version for grown-ups. Although it is probably most successfully played early in the day before taste buds have been assaulted by an army of food, cigarettes, drink, cigars and sweets, the game is unlikely to attract many participants until the midnight hour. Even then, only the foolhardy play with any enthusiasm.

Take six glasses and fill with various liquids, some disgusting, some potable. These might include used dishwater, washing-up liquid, cold tea, Ribena mixed with whisky, baby formula milk, interspersed with normal drinks such as Coca-Cola, vodka (with or without mixer), wine and fruit juices.

Each player takes it in turn to be blindfolded and sample the beverages. The one who correctly guesses the most (or isn't sick) wins.

Cheat

Another favourite which most people will know of old but, just in case some readers have missed out on the joys of authorized skullduggery, here's how to play.

Two packs of cards, complete or incomplete, are roughly dealt out to all players. It is possible to play with one pack, but it is not nearly so much fun. The aim is to get rid of your cards as quickly as possible by fair means or foul – preferably the latter. As you will have guessed already, being the dealer is an advantage – just deal one or two extra cards surreptitiously to other players.

The player on the left of the dealer starts by laying face down as many cards as he wants and declaring what he has played – for instance, 'Two 5s'. The other players follow in turn by laying *more* cards of the same value, or any number of the next value up. Two 5s could be followed by three or four 5s, or by one or more 6s, each person declaring his play, *regardless of what they have actually laid*.

A player may be challenged by anyone before the next player has taken his turn. A successful challenge means the cheat picks the entire pile of discards up; an unsuccessful challenger gets the same punishment.

The secret is to be as subtle as possible when laying your cards, and as straight-faced as possible when lying through your teeth about what you have laid.

Musical Cushions

A silly game for the fit and rough. As in the chair version, place one fewer cushions on the floor than there are players. One quick-thinking player will agree to man the 'music centre'. When the music starts, players dance around the cushions; when it stops, each player races to stake his claim to a cushion with his bum. One player will be left out, and is out of the game; one cushion is removed. It can get very physical.

Pass the Bottle

This sounds dreadful, and indeed many people will think it is. However, for those who don't mind a bit of slapstick, it can be extremely amusing.

Two teams are formed, ideally of six people each. Two bottles are placed upright on the floor. One person from each team comes forward to clasp the bottle between his knees, and then passes it to the knees of the next team member, and so on until the end of the line is reached, the winning team being the first to do so. No hands are allowed. A dropped bottle must be picked up again with the knees.

Short, tight skirts are a definite handicap, and you'd be amazed how one's knees get in the way, especially when there is a considerable difference in leg lengths. For this reason, be sure that teams are a good mix of the short and the tall.

Feet and Legs Competition

Requiring a certain amount of energy, this is best played before the third nightcap. It also requires a certain degree of confidence in your plates and pins.

A screen – a blanket or sheet will do – is stretched between two points, leaving enough space between its bottom edge and the floor through which to see ankles and feet or legs from the knee downwards, depending on which version you play. Half the participants leave the room; the other half remove their shoes, boots, socks, tights, stockings, spats, or whatever hosiery they are wearing, and line up behind the screen. The others return and attempt, in turn, to identify the owner of each pair of feet or legs. He or she who makes the most correct identifications wins.

But the point is less to win than to cause outrage and indignation. For this reason, however sexist it may sound, it works best when the party is divided up according to gender.

Vampire in the Dark

A more imaginative version of Murder in the Dark, which I have excluded on the grounds of inherent dullness, Vampire in the Dark does not rely on short-lived thrills in the dark followed by an interminable post-mortem. Rather, the thrills can last for ever, no questions asked.

Take from a pack of cards as many cards as there are players, being sure to include the Ace of Spades. Make a fan of these and let each person draw one card. He who gets the Ace of Spades must instantly grow long sharp teeth. Usually, the lights are turned off, everyone shuts their eyes and creeps as quietly as possible to a safe corner. However, the vampire is on the blood-path, his aim to convert everyone to his liquid diet by biting them on the neck! Once bitten, you too become a vampire and set off in search of new recruits. Two vampires biting each other in the dark cancel each other out and become mortal again, with the exception of the original holder of the Ace of Spades.

A high conversion rate of mortals into vampires and back again ensures a long night of high jinks.

Honest Injun

This can be played without moving from the dinner table. Just push the debris into the middle, and deal one card face down to each player. No one must peek at his card. The dealer calls out, 'Honest Injun', whereupon everybody picks up his card and holds it face out to his forehead. All players now bet on whether their own cards are higher or lower than the others'. When everyone has bet, the dealer counts to three and everyone indicates which way he has bet by sticking his thumb up or down. Winner takes all. In the event of there being a highest and lowest winner, the pot is split.

Guaranteed to infuriate real poker players, it can nevertheless provide a healthy pot. I once walked in on a serious and deadly poker game, persuaded the players to grant me one round of this frivolous game and, much to their collective fury, walked off with £20. As they had been so snooty about it, I did not give them the opportunity to win it back.

Chicken Feed

Another post-prandial game, but one that gets quite boisterous, so clear the table of anything precious and don't use your favourite pack of cards.

Spread the cards face up on the table. One person is the umpire, who sits with his back to the cards to avoid favouritism. He calls out a card. Everybody then scans the table for it. The first player to spot it pounces on it with a forefinger, dragging it back to his place. Of course, as soon as his finger lands on the card, it will be joined by many other greedy forefingers all determined to make off with the prize.

Successful players use a combination of brute strength and skilful manoeuvring and jiggling of the card. The winner is he who captures most cards. Anyone using more than one finger or applying elbow techniques to his neighbours is instantly disqualified. Cards that tear in half are void.

Piglets

All that is needed here is a blindfold and a bunch of very silly people.

After one player is blindfolded the rest sit in a circle around him. He searches out a lap on which he plonks himself, shouting, 'Squeak, piggy, squeak!' The unfortunate victim must make loud piglet noises, as if he were just about to be made into a sausage. If the blindfolded player identifies him, they swap places. If the guess is wrong, another lap is sought.

Imitations

If even a moderately good dinner has been enjoyed by the party, this game is unlikely to last very long. It is similar to Cardinal Puff (see p. 63), but even simpler and sillier.

Players stand in a circle, and one leads off by doing something like sticking his tongue out. The player on his right (this confuses people because they are more used to playing to their left) copies this and adds his own action, say, touching his toes. The third player would stick out his tongue, touch his toes, and perhaps pull his ear lobe. If by any chance you complete a round, the first player must add a new action. And so it continues, until there are so many actions to perform that remembering the sequence seems impossible, or you all fall over. The winner is likely to be young and sober, or old and sober – sober, anyway.

Stork's Nest

Another of those games which you are most likely to play when you are least fit to do so, it is a classic still-sitting-round-the table-hours-later game. All you need is an empty wine bottle and a box of matches.

Give every player twenty or so matches. The first player carefully places a match across the top of the bottle. Each subsequent player does the same, creating in the process an extraordinary and precarious edifice that does, indeed, look just like a stork's nest. The object is to get rid of all your matches. Should your match fall into the bottle (only likely to happen in the early stages), all of the players give a match from their own piles. Should your match cause the entire nest to topple from its perch, you get the whole lot, so a steady hand and nerves of steel are an asset.

You'll be amazed at how big this nest can become with strategic and daring placing of matches. As the nest grows, matches can be stuck in almost vertically rather than laid horizontally. You can make it virtually impossible for the next player to continue without causing an avalanche of matches by balancing yours in such a way that wherever he tries to position his spells disaster. It is also possible to gang up on a complacent player who has only three matches left – but it is very difficult and often backfires. Some players use two other matches, held in a V, to put a match on the nest, but I find this a great deal harder than using fingers.

Botticelli on the Forehead

This is known simply as Botticelli among sixties' children, and it does bear a close resemblance to the original game of that name (see p. 1).

Sitting round the table, everyone writes on a scrap of paper the name of a famous person, fictional or real, and passes it to the neighbour on the left, who must put it straight up to his forehead *without looking at it*. The person elected to start turns to the person on his left and endeavours to find out who he is by asking questions that can only be answered by 'Yes' or 'No'. A 'Yes' means he gets another go, a 'No' that the play moves on round the table. In this way, even an apparently simple question such as 'Am I dead?' might not get you very far, since if the answer is 'No' you will have to wait until play has come all the way back to you before you can capitalize on the fact that you know you are alive!

Participants are known to get excited and frustrated in equal measure as their chance of discovering their identity slips away from them once again.

CHAPTER 6

ONCE-OFF (AND OFTEN CRUEL)

It will quickly become clear why this chapter is called 'Once-Off'. Either the games are based on trickery and deception, which once revealed cannot be repeated with the same people, or they are simply so unpleasant that you would be in very real danger of losing your friends if you forced them to play more than once.

Spoons

A sort of distant relation of Are You There, Moriarty? (see p. 62), this requires two players, one of whom should have never played this before, an umpire and an audience, the last two being almost more important than the players.

The two participants kneel facing each other, each with a spoon handle in his mouth, and the umpire stands next to them. They take it in turns to hit the bowed head of the other once as hard as possible with the spoon. This does not hurt at all, since it is impossible to exert any force with the spoon in the mouth.

However, the player who has never played this before is actually being hit quite hard by the umpire, who has secreted his own spoon behind his back. This player's astonishment at the impact of the spoon on his head, and his redoubled efforts to inflict equal pain on his opponent, constitute the delights of the game. It can go on until the audience takes pity on the sucker, or until, in rare cases, he guesses that all is not quite as it seems.

If You Can't Do This . . .

If You Can't Do This . . .

This can drive people from the room, screaming with frustration. One person starts by rhythmically tapping the table or his knees while chanting, 'If you can't do this, you can't do anything at all.' The next person follows suit and so on around the room. As each person repeats the chant and tapping, he is told by the first player whether he has done it correctly or not. Obviously everybody thinks the precise rhythm of the tapping is the key to success – and equally obviously, it is not.

The first player has quietly and subtly introduced an extra element to the words and tapping. It might be a soft clearing of the throat, a slight inclination of the head, or a blink of the eyelid (provided you're not playing with people with a chronic blink or people having trouble with contact lenses) or whatever. This sound or movement is the key to success.

As the number of people who have twigged increases, so

does the paranoia of those still getting it wrong. By the time only one person is excluded from the club, mounting panic and feelings of isolation ensure that he will probably never become a member.

Imagine a room with fifty people all yelling 'If you can't do this, you can't do anything at all!' at one poor soul. It may sound extreme, but this did happen at an art school's end-of-term bash. The girl in question bolted from the room, gibbering, 'No, I can't, I *can't*.' More usually played in smaller groups, it need not be so cruel, but it can still convince perfectly intelligent people that they are being as thick as a Sumo wrestler's thigh.

X-ray Eyes

For this trick you provide all players with a piece of paper and an opaque envelope. Ask each of them to write down a word or two, such as Red Rum, Chimney Pot, Olympic Games, fold the paper and seal it in the envelope, making sure it cannot possibly be read through it.

You then collect the envelopes. Taking the top one, you make a great show of staring at it, feeling it, 'sensing' the words written therein. After a lot of this sort of palaver, you hesitantly begin to show signs of revelation. 'I see a horse,' you might say. 'A race, jumps, winning, yes . . . yes . . . it's coming . . . I *think* it's the name of a horse . . . Red Rum? *Yes!* It's Red Rum, I'm certain. Did anyone write "Red Rum"?'

To the assembled company's surprise and grudging admiration, someone admits that he did. Casually opening the envelope, you check the piece of paper and place it behind you, and move onto the next envelope. Repeating your award-winning performance and spiel, you again make a correct divination. And on it goes, to the rising astonishment of the group, as you get them all right!

If you haven't already guessed how this is done, read on.

One member of the group is your accomplice, with

whom you have agreed a phrase beforehand, in this case, Red Rum. When you collect the envelopes, make sure his is at the bottom of the pile. Obviously, the contents of this envelope are all you know, and will have to be the answer to the first envelope. At this point you hope the audience will assume you have special powers, and not demand to check the piece of paper. Having opened and read the first envelope, it should be plain sailing, as you 'divine' the contents of each successive envelope with the knowledge of what was written in the previous one. When you have finished, make sure to muddle the papers before handing them over to any would-be sleuth who has the cheek to doubt your powers.

Find the Person

One person leaves the room, declaring that he will be able to identify any person in the room whom the others care to nominate. Again, an accomplice is required, whose role it is to direct the guesser to the identity of the Chosen One. This the accomplice does by imitating the stance of the Chosen One. On coming back into the room, the guesser makes great play of thinking hard until finally pointing to the right person.

Should the accomplice and the Chosen One be one and the same, a simple code to let the guesser know will have been worked out beforehand between him and the accomplice, who might, for example, pick his nose or yawn.

The watchers aim to work out how the identification is achieved, and the game can continue until everybody has succeeded in doing this. Alternatively, as people guess they can take turns with the accomplice.

There are many different versions of this game, such as Are We in Cahoots? and Find the Object. They all work along the same principle of two players being in the know, the others in the dark. Any code can be used, and indeed you will find that different families have often worked out their own.

Likes and Dislikes

This game is likely to be played just the once, except by rhino-hides, not because of any trickery, but rather because after just one round it becomes too personal for comfort.

Sitting round the dinner table, each person in turn has to declare to the person on his right what physical attribute he particularly likes about him or her. But he also has to declare which one he hates, such as, 'I love the backs of your knees, but I hate your face.'

When everyone has made a declaration, the leader or host announces that each person must kiss the feature he hated, and bite the one he liked – another reason why this is a once-off.

The Dream Game

The aim here is to convince one person that he is more intimately known to his friends than he could possibly have imagined. One person leaves the room having been told that the others will invent a dream – an accurate one – that they think he is likely to have had. On returning, the 'dreamer' tries to guess the invented dream by asking questions – which can only be answered by 'Yes', 'No' or 'Maybe'.

Of course, no dream has actually been made up. The 'inventors' have merely decided on a private system by which to answer the dreamer's questions. For instance, everyone will answer 'Yes' to any question in which the last word ends in any letter of the alphabet from A to M; 'No' if the last word ends in N or any letter thereafter; and 'Maybe' for a word ending in Y.

This can go on for ages. As the dream is built, answer by answer, the 'dreamer' becomes more and more intrigued as to how his friends *knew* such things about him. Inevitably, the dreamer will ask questions that reveal ever more about himself. The murky depths are plumbed – to the general merriment of everyone else.

I remember a time when a friend vowed never to touch a drop again, convinced that she must have babbled in drink – or talked in her sleep – or that the entire assembled company had perused her most private diary. Of course, it was she who had told us, and most interesting it was too!

Lonely Hearts

A very simple but surprisingly revealing game, best played by a group of friends – but a stranger in their midst can only add spice!

As the name implies, it is based on the contact ads placed by those looking for partners in magazines and newspapers such as *Time Out* magazine in London, *Private Eye, New Statesman* and *Gay Times*. Take your pick or invent your own.

Each person writes a short advert describing any other person in the room and an *imaginary* partner he or she might be seeking. It is not the intention to pair off those present – the exercise is quite controversial enough without rearranging the natural couplings which will probably be in evidence. The ads are then put into a container and shuffled around. In turn, each person picks one out and reads it to the assembled lonely hearts (it doesn't matter two hoots if you pick out the one you wrote), the others guessing to whom it refers. If a winner is needed, it is the person who guesses correctly most often, or who is deemed to have written the wittiest and most accurate advert, but I doubt whether winning will be an issue here.

When played amongst friends, the game naturally gets personal – and therefore dangerous – but all the more interesting for it. Descriptions can be based either on the writer's perception of his subject or on how he thinks his subject might describe himself. The secret is to stick to basic facts about a person, but glamorize them amusingly. For instance, a country solicitor who happens to own one small pony and a couple of acres, and occasionally goes abroad on judicial business might be described as:

'Land-owning, hunting, globe-trotting member of the international legal fraternity, who likes to tell a good yarn and to drink fine wines, seeks . . .'

Supplying a description of an imaginary partner for your subject can cause as much disturbance to hitherto unruffled friendships as Analogies (see p. 27).

Alternatively, if skins are thin, or tempers are likely to fray quickly, or you are playing with relative strangers, a coward's option is to choose celebrities, preferably recently in the news, as your subjects. This is still fun, but blunts the edge of what can otherwise be a viciously cutting and entertaining game.

Honeymoon

Like others in this chapter, Honeymoon relies on the the main participants being ignorant of the rules, and is chiefly entertaining for the spectators.

A couple, preferably not close friends and ideally an unlikely partnership, are dispatched from the room. On return, they are asked to perform some seemingly pointless, but potentially physically awkward activity. This could be both of them climbing into the same small cardboard box or carrier bag. Given the unfeasibility of what they have been asked to do and their natural diffidence, the ensuing conversation should be replete with such innocuous remarks as:

'Squeeze up a bit.'

'Watch out! Your knee's in my groin.'

'If you move your left leg, I could get my arm underneath your . . .'

'Hang on to my shoulder, and I'll pull you up (in, over, etc.).'

They, of course, have no idea at all why they are carrying out this absurd task, nor why the audience is laughing fit to bust. And it is because their helpful advice to each other is being heard by the others as a first-night-of-the-honeymoon conversation!

Reactions to being let in on the secret vary from utter contempt to bashfulness to righteous indignation at being made a laughing-stock. It may sound childishly smutty but given the right combination of people it can be very funny.

Animal Charades

Another game for the spectators' amusement. Put into a hat the same number of bits of paper as there are players, on each of which you have written the *same* animal: frog works well. Each person then picks out a scrap, keeping its contents *strictly* secret. When everyone has memorized his animal, select one victim, send him out of the room, explaining that he is the first to act out his animal (miming only, for obvious reasons) and should have time to compose himself, think about it, get another drink, powder his nose . . . whatever, *but get rid of him.*

Meanwhile, you explain to the others that frog was written on *all* the pieces of paper, and they must not guess frog! You might be thinking, what's the point? Well, you'd be astonished at the length of time someone will spend hopping around the room froggily, and more and more frenziedly, while the audience shouts, 'Kangaroo', 'Bunny', 'Wallaby', 'Grasshopper'.

How Many Matches?

An accomplice is not necessary but can be used to confuse matters further in what is another trick game.

One player takes as many matches as he likes, tosses them on to a table or the floor, and asks, 'How many matches?' The audience will answer literally, and on the face of it correctly, since it is not difficult to count the number of matches thrown. Of course, they are not really being asked to count the matches, but the number of fingers the thrower subtly extends just after he has let go of the matches and before he sweeps them up again. To confuse spectators you can obviously extend the same number of fingers as matches thrown to start with.

This bald description may make the game sound very monotonous, but, as with other tricks, people become obsessed with working out the 'rule'. The thrower usually gets mighty bored and announces he will explain, whereupon everyone else shouts, 'No, no, just one more go! I think I've got it!' In the end, whenever that is, everyone does get it.

Russian Omelette

The expression 'being left with egg on your face' must surely derive from this mean and embarrassing game – or some clever-clogs invented the game to go with the expression. What, of course, it really is is a non-fatal version of Russian roulette.

Well in advance, hard boil one fewer eggs than there are people. Allow them to cool, even putting them in the fridge so that there is no hint of warmth from their shells. Get everyone to sit round a table, in the centre of which you have placed all the hardboiled eggs – plus a raw one. Ho ho!

One by one, everyone takes an egg and cracks it hard on the top of his head with a sigh of relief if the shell merely cracks, or a great river of dribbling slime if it's the raw one. Tension mounts almost unbearably as egg after solid egg is cracked. If you are unfortunate enough to be the last person and no raw egg has so far been turned up, you must still crack that last egg. By now it is a question of damage limitation, and you might try to get away with cracking it on your forehead.

Of course, leaving the eggs to be picked randomly means you risk the first egg being the raw one, and it is doubtful whether you'd get anyone to play again. To avoid this, place the eggs round the table, making sure the raw one is over half-way round. You'll have to do this with some degree of subtlety if you don't want to arouse

Russian Omelette

suspicions, particularly if you want to target a particular victim.

Bananas

When you're well and truly fed up with someone, and your sole desire is to humiliate them without pain, try this.

Suggest a game of Bananas, explaining briefly that all it involves is three blindfolded players racing to eat a banana each. When you have whittled down the multitude of volunteers to three, somehow take two aside and explain the real 'game' to them.

Blindfold the victim and give him a banana, and pretend to do the same to your two accomplices. On the word 'Go' the victim will desperately gobble his banana, shoving it into his mouth, believing he is taking part in a race. Exhortation and encouragement can be supplied by the spectators – 'Go on, go on!', 'You're winning!', 'Hurry, you're nearly there!' When he has finally swallowed and probably almost choked on the fruit, and the spectators are

Bananas

all applauding enthusiastically, he whips off his blindfold to
discover everyone grinning – and bananaless. Yes, he has
been fooled!

CHAPTER 7

MISCELLANEOUS

This chapter is a mishmash of games which do not comfortably fit in other categories, but which it would be a pity to exclude. Many of them require props – cards or dice, one even a full-sized billiard table, another old Christmas cards – others are rather active, outdoorsy games. Play them where and when you will.

Wink Murder

This is an unexpectedly suspenseful game, which can induce nervous giggling in some players, rather like watching a thriller.

Players sit round a table and draw a card from a handful which must include the Ace of Spades and which must not number more than there are players. He who draws the Ace of Spades is the murderer – a fact he must keep well to himself. Now the game begins.

The murderer kills by catching the eye of another player and shoots a deadly wink in his direction. The victim waits a few seconds before slumping over dead. Anyone else intercepting the wink can reveal the identity of the murderer, and a new round of cards is dealt.

This is an extraordinarily quiet game. The silence contributes to the mounting tension as players attempt to avoid direct eye contact with each other, but at the same time want to catch the murderer in the act. Staring intently at the table will get you nowhere – you'll just be the last victim.

Racing Demon

Racing Demon

An old favourite for all ages, this timeless card game is included because it is just such enormous fun, and requires no special skill at cards. Do not use good cards.

It is best played with at least four people, although I have been party to chaotic games of ten players. The game should be played round a large table, or on the floor with players forming a roomy circle. Each player has a pack of cards (whose backs *must* be different). First he deals himself a pile of thirteen cards face down, known as the talon, which he then turns over (the pile is now face up). Next, he deals four cards face up, placing them in a line in front of him (the depot). The remaining cards (the hand) are held face down in the hand. When all players have reached this stage, the game can begin.

As the name suggests, this is a race, and a rough one to boot. The ultimate aim is to get rid of your talon, at the same time as getting as many cards as possible into the middle, from your hand, depot and talon. On the word

'Go', players scan their visible cards (the four in the depot and the one on top of the talon), slamming into the centre any visible Aces. These now become common property on which any player can build, following suit, from Ace to King. Even if you don't immediately have an Ace, you may be able to bang a 2 on to someone else's Ace.

Cards removed from the depot are replaced from the talon. The cards in your hand are turned over as fast as possible in threes. You may only ever play the top card of these batches of three. You may *never* pick the ones underneath. The same applies to the talon – only the top card can be played. When you have 'turned' your whole hand, you pick it up, turn it over and start again.

The depot is also used to 'free' cards from your hand or talon, by building numerically and in alternate colours (so, a black 10 can be put on a red Knave, etc.). Although this is a useful device for reducing your talon and ensuring that the batches of three change, players should beware of trapping cards, particularly as the piles in the middle get nearer completion. Again, only the last card in the sequence can be played.

Sometimes, and usually in small games, the flow of cards into the middle completely dries up. At this point, by mutual consent, all players can move the top card of their hand to the bottom in order to get the game going again. You are *not* allowed to do this simply because your hand has become stuck.

As the game hots up, cards are slapped into the middle with ever-increasing ferocity. Two players often aim to place the next card in the sequence at the same time, and vicious squabbles can break out. The player who thinks he was first shouts 'Mine!'. If the competition does not retreat voluntarily, both players should keep their fingers on their cards, the game is stopped and the other players adjudicate.

A player who completes a pile with a King bellows 'King!' and removes it from the centre. The first person to get rid of his talon bellows 'Out!' and the game stops immediately. All the cards in the middle, including any

King piles that may have been removed, are turned face down and sorted into their respective packs. Each player then counts his own cards, subtracting from the total the number left in his talon, and adding five for each King won. The person who went out obviously has nothing to subtract, and adds ten for being first out. Cards remaining in the depot are not counted.

Packs are shuffled and passed to the left. The winner of the previous round adds one extra card to his talon. Should the same brilliant practitioner win again, he adds another. When he stops winning he can only reduce the number of cards in his talon by one card each round.

Racing Demon can go on for hours as it is particularly addictive. Limits can be set either by playing a set number of rounds, with the highest scorer winning, or by playing to a predetermined score, say 300, with the first to reach it winning.

There are ways of cheating too numerous to mention, and indeed I am afraid to say there are people who are compulsive Racing Demon cheats, who have to be watched with an eagle eye and often and sharply reprimanded. My mother is one of these and still manages to lose most of the time. On the other hand, a vicar of my acquaintance is an accomplished and noisy cheat who wins more often than not.

Compulsion

Compulsion is a betting game for which you need five dice and chips (matches, pennies or pound coins will do), and pencil and paper, but which is not complicated. It relies on risking your all on a high or low bet and sticking to it through five rolls of dice.

One person is elected dealer and he sits on one side of a table facing the other players. Each player is given fifteen chips, the dealer keeping enough with which to honour any debts. He writes the name of each player at the top of a piece of paper, on which he will keep track of their betting and scoring.

The first player, on the left of dealer, starts the game by throwing all five dice together. He then chooses to go high or low on this roll, the dealer recording which way he went and how much he has bet (usually written in brackets alongside). He then passes the dice on, and play proceeds around the table.

When everyone has had one turn, the dealer removes one of the dice from play and gives the remaining four to the first player, who rolls them as before. At the end of each subsequent round, the dealer removes another die, the last round being played with just the one. Players bet high or low on each throw, the dealer recording these bets and scores. There have been five rounds – or something's gone wrong.

Now the dealer adds each player's scores. A score between 11 and 24 disqualifies the player – a range that is all too easy to fall into. Twenty-five or more and 10 or less are winning scores, the amount of winnings determined by further dice rolling. At this point the dealer ascribes to each remaining player a 'Pay-off Number' between 1 and 6. This is an entirely arbitrary process and he could, should he choose to do so, assign all players the same number, say 3. Each player throws all five dice again, hoping, in this case, for as many 3s as possible, because each 3 wins him his stake again. If no 3s appear in his throw, the dealer takes his stake. Another way of giving players their Pay-off Numbers is simply to number them 1 to 6 around the table.

Pinochle and *Band Switch*

The competitiveness and maliciousness involved in both versions of this game make it a perversely pleasurable game to play.

It is best played with two packs of cards and at least six people. Each person is dealt seven cards, the dealer placing the remaining pile face down in the centre of the floor or table and turning the top card face up next to it. This is the discard pile.

The object is to get rid of your cards, at the same time as gunning for other players by clever use of certain 'special' cards which subtly alter the game. The player on the left of the dealer starts by throwing a card from his hand, which must follow suit or be of the same face value as the card the dealer turned up (i.e. if the first card is a 7 of Clubs, a player must lay a 7 or any Club). If he cannot do this he must take a card from the stock pile. He may play this card if he can. Play continues round the table, each player throwing one card from his hand according to the dictates of the card on top of the discard pile. This seems boringly straightforward, but now the 'specials' come into play: an Ace changes the direction of play from clockwise to anti-clockwise or vice versa; an 8 jumps a player; a Queen can be accompanied by any other cards of the *same* suit in that go; a Jack can be played in lieu of any card except a 2; a 2 must be followed by another 2 (a card of the same suit does *not* work here). If a player cannot play a 2 he has to pick up two penalty cards from the stock pile. On the other hand, if he can the next player also has to play a 2, failing which he has to take four cards. And so on – for each consecutive 2 that is played the penalty for a player who cannot follow with a 2 is two extra cards. As soon as a player fails to follow with a 2 and picks the penalty cards, normal play resumes.

The slightest hesitation or false move in response to one of the 'special' cards results in immediate cries of 'Penalty!', gaining you yet another extra card. When a player gets down to his last card, he is supposed to shout 'Pinochle!' (pronounced peaknuckle), before anyone else notices he has only one card left and shouts 'Penalty!'. Should this happen, all the other players will be out to get you (by strategically playing their 8s and Jacks). Deviousness is the name of this game, so if you can subtly hide the fact that you are about to win, all the better.

BAND SWITCH

Rumoured to have been first played by a pop group in the

Moon and Sixpence public house, Hanwell, Oxfordshire, this is a tougher and crueller variation. Penalties abound, and no mercy is shown to those who hesitate or make a mistake.

The two bossiest players form a *Court* who decide penalties and settle arguments. They are likely to be the two people who have played this version before.

When a player cannot play, in addition to picking an extra card, he must also shout 'Pass' loudly and clearly as soon as he has checked that he cannot play the card he has picked. Failure to say 'Pass', or mumbling it, incurs another penalty card.

As in Pinochle, *hesitation* or *inappropriate responses* incur penalties, but the Court may well award you two or even three cards (instead of just the one) if you hesitate for too long – a length of time which is quite arbitrary.

If you have more than seven cards in your hand, and it's all rather confusing, you may shout out 'Time to consider', which will earn you a moment's respite. You cannot do this after hesitating even slightly, otherwise you will end up with three penalty cards.

Should you need to replenish your glass, collect your thoughts or go to the loo, you are allowed to say 'Time out' (loudly and clearly, of course), at which point all players down cards. Failure to announce your intention to take leave is punished by at least two penalty cards.

In this version you cannot disguise the fact that you're about to *go out*, since you must knock three times loudly on the floor or table when you're down to your last card. Failure to do so gains an extra card.

Swearing, *talking too much* and *arguing* with the Court are all high-risk activities and will be punished accordingly.

Tempers can be lost irretrievably in the thicket of emotion this game engenders. Seldom does anyone accept a penalty card without argument; paranoia creeps in as friends round on you; malice can take over from healthy competition – all in all, you are unlikely to be speaking to each other at the end of a few rounds of this.

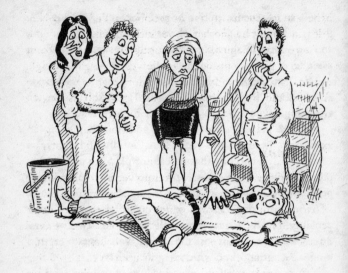

Kick the Bucket

At the end of both Pinochle and Band Switch, five
points are awarded for any 'special' cards, one for any
others left in your hand, the winner being the one with the
fewest points – and friends.

Kick the Bucket

This is really an outdoors game, but it can be played in
houses with two staircases – which probably limits the
occasions on which you can indulge in what is, at bottom,
a noisy, exhausting, but at the same time exhilarating,
version of Tag. Failing two staircases, a back and a front
door, and perhaps a ground-floor window large enough to
escape through, will do.

A bucket or tin can is placed at a strategic point in the
house. It's best if it can be equidistant from each staircase. One
person is elected 'he', who counts to fifty while the others
hide. His purpose is to catch as many players as possible, and

as he does so, send his captives to the bucket. They can only be released from it by another player kicking it hard.

As you can imagine, he has a tiring and frustrating time of it, so if played outside, he is allowed to 'catch' by sight rather than touch, and if there are more than eight players there should be two hes. Beware of heart-attacks in the over-45s.

Lions

This is another completely knackering version of Tag which again should be played outdoors or in a house with plenty of escape routes. When caught by the 'Lion', the player remains in the same place and shouts 'Rescue! Rescue!' until another player comes to his aid. A wily Lion, however, may well hang around, surreptitiously waiting to make another kill. If the caught player sees the Lion returning he must immediately change his cry, trying to indicate a roar, 'Rrrrr-rrrr', so as to warn his approaching rescuer.

A player can only ever be rescued by touch, but as in Kick the Bucket (see above), the Lion may 'catch' by sight if you are playing outside.

Freda

This game is best played when the company is fired by alcohol and enthusiasm (or anything, really). However, you will still find opportunities limited as a full-sized billiard table is an absolute necessity, and many country houses and hotels which possess such a thing strictly forbid the playing of Freda on them. The spoilsports.

Just in case you're lucky enough to find a sympathetic host with a table, here's how it's done (not including individual house rules).

The object of the game is simply to keep a red snooker ball moving by hitting it with the white cue ball. Before starting, establish order of play and the number of lives (usually three) allotted to each player. The red ball is placed on the black spot or pink spot of the table, the white at the other end. Play begins with the first player bowling the white ball down the table to hit the red ball. He has three attempts to do this, and should he fail on the last he loses a life and play moves to the next player. Some establishments rule that a player cannot lose his last life in this way. If he fails on this third attempt to hit the red ball, it is moved further up the table until he hits it.

Once the red ball has been hit and is on the move, players take it in turns to seize the white ball and roll it onto the red, *always* playing from alternate ends of the table, never the sides. Any player who fails to hit the red ball before it comes to a stop, loses a life. Each player has three attempts to hit the red ball, losing a life if he fails on the third, even if the red ball is still moving.

Lives are lost also for playing out of turn, from the sides, from the wrong end, for causing one or both balls to leap from the table, or for obstructing another player. If one player pots the red, the next player loses a life, which is a useful way of getting at those who never seem to lose them by any other means. Potting the white ball carries no penalty, and play continues without pause.

Played properly, Freda is a fast game, with over-heated players rushing round the table, screaming and swearing, swinging round the corners by holding on to the cushions, and often, in their excitement, flinging the white ball on to the slate. It is for these reasons that serious snooker and billiards players regard it in the same light as poker players see Honest Injun (see p. 77).

Burning Money

In these non-smoking times, this will seem like a very old-fashioned and politically incorrect game. I have racked my brains to come up with an alternative to the now-loathed gasper – but nothing else burns in quite the same way.

Stretch a piece of paper (of the ordinary typing or writing kind) over a glass or jam jar and secure it with an elastic band. Place a coin in the centre of the paper, and light a cigarette. Each person takes it in turns to burn a hole in the paper around the coin, the loser being he who causes the coin to fall into the glass.

If you have enjoyed this, you may start again.

Walking, Courting or One, Two, Three, Pass

For each player you need four cards of the same face value, so, for example, if there were six players you might take from a pack, all the Aces, Kings, 8s, 5s, 3s and 2s. Shuffle these and deal them out. The cards must not be looked at before the deal is complete. Players sit round a table or in a circle on the floor. Place something snatchable, such as a pepper-pot, in the middle.

The object is to collect four cards of the same face value by passing one card to the left and receiving one from the right. There are four stages: Walking, Courting, Banns Up and Marriage. Some modern versions include a fifth stage: Divorce. After declaring Banns Up, a player cannot speak until he is married: failure to keep silent and it's back to the singles bars.

After the players have looked at their cards and decided which to pass, they all say together, 'One, Two, Three, Pass', and do so. They continue until one, or as is often the case everybody at the same time, gets a complete set, whereupon they pounce for the pepper-pot, the first one to get it shouting, 'Walking!' They then start again in Courting mode, and the game continues until someone gets to the altar.

Old Maid

The object of this game is to not end up as the 'old maid' – the person left with a Queen.

A pack of cards is dealt, from which one Queen has

been removed. Each player discards any pairs he has in his hand. Then, starting from the dealer's left, each player, in turn, takes a card from the fanned-out cards of the person on his right. If the card he takes makes up a pair he can then discard them, and so on, with the person with the solitary Queen desperately willing someone to take it from him. Sometimes the Queen is passed from person to person with alarming speed, each player trying to keep a deadpan expression so as not to give away her whereabouts.

Zilch

This is a compulsive game for risk-takers: the more you play the more you need to play – just one more round might net you that elusive high score. Don't be put off by what follows – it is a game far harder to explain than it is to play.

You need six numbered dice, pencil and paper with which to score, and, as the method of scoring is quite complicated, an *aide-mémoire* of the value of the dice. So, before reading further, copy out the following:

Plus scores

Each 5   = 50
Each 1   = 100
Three 2s = 200
Three 3s = 300
Three 4s = 400
Three 5s = 500
Three 6s = 600
Three 1s = 1000
Three pairs (of any number) = 1000
A run of 1 to 6 = 1500
Six 6s = outright win at any stage

Minus scores

When throwing with *two* or *four* dice, pairs, except 5s and 1s which score as singles, are negative scorers:

Two 2s = − 200
Two 3s = − 300
Two 4s = − 400
Two 6s = − 600
All six dice thrown without a plus score = − 1000
Five dice thrown without a plus score = − 500,
regardless of what your first die was (1 or 5)

The object of the game is to be the first to score a mutually
and arbitrarily agreed number of points, say 6000. Throw
one die to see who starts, the highest scorer going first.
Then, each player takes it in turn to throw all six dice. Any
dice, such as a 1 or a 5, or three of a kind, which have a
plus score are put to one side and the player continues with
the remaining dice. A plus score must show in order to
gain a further throw. He may choose to stick on a fairly
modest score, rather than risk losing that turn's score by
'zilching', that is failing to throw a plus score with the
remaining dice − remember that five or six dice thrown
without a plus score become a minus score (see above).
Play then passes to the next player. A player's turn also
ends when he throws minus-scoring dice.

It is important to note that within a player's turn any
minus points scored take precedence over any plus points
(which become void) and are subtracted from his running
total.

Should a player successfully manage to score on all six
dice, he must 'turn' them, i.e. throw all six again. You
cannot stick on six dice (unless, of course, you have
achieved the near impossible trick of throwing six 6s).

You do not have to set aside all your scoring dice. If you
threw a 5 and three of a kind and set them all aside, you
would be running a high risk of not throwing a plus score
with the remaining two − or, even worse, of throwing a
minus-scoring pair. Removing just the 5 from play gives
you a greater chance of throwing a scoring combination in
the remaining five dice. Of course, if you failed to show
any score, you'd have clocked up − 500.

As the target score is neared, if you are down the order of the play, i.e. playing fifth or sixth in a game of six players, it is advisable to keep your number of points below the winning score. This is because everyone has to have the same number of turns. So, if the first or second player reaches the target, say by scoring 6200, you then have a turn in hand and with clever use of your scoring dice can score more, say 6300, in which case you win.

The constant lure of amassing a vast plus score, coupled with the ever-present fear of losing the lot by throwing minus scores, makes Zilch a thrillingly addictive game which can go on over a whole weekend.

Liar Dice

Here is another dice game, but a poker-based gambling one which can be played with either poker or numbered dice. If playing with the latter, 1 equals the Ace, and 6 to 2 represent King to 9 in descending order.

Each player is given three betting units – matches, counters, pennies, £5 notes or whatever you like – and throws one die to see who starts (Ace is high if you are playing with poker dice). Although any number of people may play, the game only ever really takes place between two players.

The first player rolls all six dice, hiding them with a cupped hand from the other players. He announces a poker hand – anything from one pair to five of a kind – to the player on his left, but the declared hand need not bear any resemblance to what he actually has. That player may accept it, in which case it becomes his turn to throw. He then throws all the dice or as many as he cares to, but he must pass to the player on *his* left a better hand than the one he received.

However, he may challenge the hand being offered to him. If his doubts are justified, the lying toad who threw first has to place one betting unit in the pot and give one to his challenger. If his doubts are groundless, and the first player was telling the gospel truth about his hand, then the doubter must put a betting unit in the pot, and the first player starts again.

Play proceeds in this fashion round the table. When a player has nothing left to bet with, he drops out of the game. The other players continue until only one player is left with anything to bet with. He is the winner and takes the pot.

Bobby's Drinking Game

This is really a pub or student bar game which can be played at home or, of course, ruinously expensively in a cocktail bar. It is fast, easy and silly, but was apparently a huge success not only in a friend's student days but also when he went to Burma, where he played it with local tribesmen. Despite the lack of a common language, and with a guide translating the numbers, a brilliant evening was spent getting sloshed on the home-brewed lychee whisky.

Say there are six drinkers, one writes down a number between nought and one hundred. Each person in turn guesses what the number is. If you are stupid enough to guess it correctly, you have to drink up and buy the next round. When played at home, a drinking forfeit is substituted. Otherwise, the game proceeds as follows: say Drinker One chooses the number sixty-nine, he turns to Drinker Two saying 'Nought to one hundred'. Drinker Two might say 'Fifty-five'. Drinker One turns to Drinker Three and says 'Fifty-five to one hundred', and so on round the drinkers, narrowing the target down.

After one circuit, Drinker One must himself narrow the target by one from either the top or bottom. For example, if the target has been narrowed to sixty-two to seventy-three, and it's Drinker One's go, he must turn to Drinker Two and say either 'Sixty-three to seventy-three' or 'Sixty-two to seventy-two'. This ensures that even the chooser of the number can lose, since if the target was narrowed to sixty-eight to seventy, he would be forced to say 'Sixty-nine'.

Drinker One can never check what number he wrote down. If he forgets when in his cups, he loses. The loser chooses the next number, and doubles all round.

Frank Muir's Dinner Parties

This is so called because Frank Muir, desperately trying to overcome a friend's tendency always to call the shots, invented it in order to win it. He didn't.

It is really not so much a game as a way of amusing one another. One person is invited to pick eight guests for the World's Most Embarrassingly Awful Dinner Party. They can come from any country, any period and be alive or dead, real or fictional. The idea is to come up with a group of people who would have absolutely nothing to say to each other. Everyone else then tries to come up with convincing reasons for these characters to get on swimmingly. Here is Frank Muir's original dinner party, round the table from left to right: Mother Theresa, Attila the Hun, Mrs Mary Whitehouse, Giacomo Casanova, Queen Victoria, Dr Crippen, Moll Flanders and Lord Curzon (two reserves were Nicholas Nickleby's mother and Terry Wogan). By anyone's standards, he felt, this would be an unmitigated disaster.

But the friend who always called the shots pointed out that: Mother Theresa and Lord Curzon would have India in common; Queen Victoria would recognize a kindred spirit in Attila the Hun; Moll Flanders could tell Dr Crippen of the delightful women he might have met in America had he got there; and Mrs Whitehouse, never one to pull her punches, would take the opportunity to lecture Casanova on the appalling example he set for posterity (though he would not be listening as he would be concentrating on playing footsie under the table with Moll).

Archbishop of York's Christmas Card Game

Here is a gentle way of passing post-Christmas afternoons and making use of all those hundreds of cards you got from people you've never heard of.

One person should write on slips of paper categories appropriate to Christmas cards, such as Fattest Robin, Ugliest Baby Jesus, Largest Number of Wings, Most Tasteless, Least Christmassy, Most Glittery, Smuttiest – whatever is suggested by your particular collection. These slips are put in a hat.

How many cards you use depends on the number you've received and the number of players – the more of both the better. You won't have much fun with six cards and three people. Deal the cards out to players who sit round a table or in a circle on the floor.

Taking it in turns, the players pick a slip of paper from the hat and read out the category on it. Each player throws a card from their hand which he thinks is most appropriate to the category. When everyone has discarded a card, players take a vote on the winner and the person who threw it gets one point. The next player then picks another slip from the hat, and so the game proceeds. Make sure you have the right categories to cover the cards in a hand.

Outburst

This is similar to Categories (see p. 40), but noisier and faster. One person compiles a list of things in a category, such as parts of the body (leg, arm, head, spleen, etc.). Fifteen would suffice for one category. He then tells the other players what the category is, and they all start shouting out names of body parts, scoring a point only when they hit on one that is on the compiler's list. At the end of a minute, the compiler scores one point for each body part missed by the others, and a new compiler suggests another category.

This has been turned into a commercial board game, but all you need is pencil and paper, and a bit of imagination.

Who? Who?

This is an 'at home' version of a panel game invented by Anthony Blond. The name of the game comes from a remark made by the Duke of Wellington to Lord Derby. At the beginning of 1852, the ageing Iron Duke had just helped Palmerston bring down Russell's government. Lord Derby was invited to form a new cabinet, Tories all, and held a reception to introduce them to the victor of Waterloo. But the crusty Duke still harboured a certain resentment towards many of them, and chose to play heavily on his chronic deafness: as Derby led them forward one by one, announcing them, Wellington roared, 'Who? Who?'

In this game contestants compete to answer clues which identify a famous person. It's an intelligent, provocative game for sharp minds and ready wits. It pits the logic of riddles and crosswords against the erudition of the scholar and historian, and the *risqué* titillation of gossip against the beady eye and elephantine memory of the true social observer.

The clues are usually both visual and verbal, depending on the forethought and preparation of the games master, and each of them refers to one of the more unlikely episodes in the subject's career.

The games master will need quite a lot of time beforehand to prepare this though, of course, it could be done in teams, but leave a lot of time as the more devious the clues the better.

Who? Who? is a team game, with two teams and, ideally, three people on each. The games master is chairman.

Each famous person can be identified from five clues, which are graded according to their difficulty, and score appropriately. Thus 10, 8, 6, 4, and 2 for the easiest. All the clues are open to the first team to answer. A wrong guess is penalized by the loss of 2 points – so it's possible for a team to end up with a minus score.

The chairman starts by reading out or showing the five clues to Team One. For example:

1. For 10 points. Who died in a colonial-style eighteenth-century mansion?
2. Right, for 8 points. To whom did a crowd of 50,000 people doff their hats when he arrived off Portsmouth?
3. For 6 points. Who left a million pounds in a bank in the Strand when he died – yet even so, was still one of the poorest members of his family?
4. For 4 points. Who made his favourite General a King?
5. For 2 points. Who is now thought to have died of arsenic poisoning?

Believe it or not, the answer is Napoléon. As I am sure you can imagine, there will be a lot of heated discussion and squabbling, but a dedicated games master can have a lot of fun making up the clues. Of course, the clues can be simplified, depending on the players.

INDEX OF GAMES